What people are saying about

TO LIVE IS CHRIST TO DIE IS GAIN

"The church has been blessed by the book of Philippians ever since Paul wrote it, and this presentation of it is fresh and powerful. Matt mines the riches of this great Bible book to teach us to never be content with stagnant Christianity."

Kyle Idleman, teaching pastor at
Southeast Christian Church and
bestselling author of *Not a Fan*

"Matt's words will kick you in the tail in the best way. We don't want to live numb, and we often need a kick to remember life isn't a game and God is no myth. You will find yourself craving God again and craving everything else a little less."

Jennie Allen, author of *Anything*

"To know Jesus is the essence of life, and I love how Matt Chandler stirs up our affections for Him in his book *To Live Is Christ, to Die Is Gain*. Matt's beautiful, practical, and straightforward unpacking of Philippians will nudge you toward maturity … and a more robust walk with the Savior. Get it, and dive in today."

Louie Giglio, pastor of Passion City Church/
Passion Conferences and author of *Indescribable*

"I trust Matt Chandler to speak on any biblical issue, but especially on discipleship. This book will help you live as Jesus would if He were in your place."

Dr. Darrin Patrick, founding pastor of the Journey and author of
For the City, Church Planter, and *The Dude's Guide to Manhood*

"Few men whom I have personally known have truly suffered. Even fewer have I known who have suffered well. Matt Chandler is one of them. Matt has written an excellent book reminding us that one of our primary callings as followers of Christ is to die to ourselves and that only through that death can we truly live."

Matt Carter, pastor of preaching and vision at the Austin
Stone Community Church and coauthor of *The Real Win*

"Matt Chandler has offered readers rich biblical wisdom in his writings thus far, and *To Live Is Christ, to Die Is Gain* is no exception. This book calls us to follow Jesus with everything we've got. It's as simple and as profound as that. This powerful new work cuts through all the trappings and goes to the heart of the gospel: Jesus. Highly recommended!"

Mark Batterson, lead pastor of National Community Church
and *New York Times* bestselling author of *The Circle Maker*

"Matt Chandler is a man captivated by Jesus, the gospel, and grace. In this, his latest book, he takes us on a journey into the depths of Paul's famous letter to the Philippians and reveals the full beauty of a life so centered on Jesus that all else pales in comparison."

Larry Osborne, pastor of North Coast
Church and author of *Sticky Church*

TO LIVE
IS CHRIST
TO DIE
IS GAIN

MATT
CHANDLER

WITH JARED C. WILSON

David C Cook
transforming lives together

TO LIVE IS CHRIST, TO DIE IS GAIN
Published by David C Cook
4050 Lee Vance View
Colorado Springs, CO 80918 U.S.A.

David C Cook Distribution Canada
55 Woodslee Avenue, Paris, Ontario, Canada N3L 3E5

David C Cook U.K., Kingsway Communications
Eastbourne, East Sussex BN23 6NT, England

The graphic circle C logo is a registered trademark of David C Cook.

The website addresses recommended throughout this book are offered as a
resource to you. These websites are not intended in any way to be or imply an
endorsement on the part of David C Cook, nor do we vouch for their content.

All Scripture quotations, unless otherwise noted, are taken from The Holy Bible,
English Standard Version® (ESV®), copyright © 2001 by Crossway, a publishing
ministry of Good News Publishers. Used by permission. All rights reserved.

LCCN 2013943293
ISBN 978-1-4347-0685-0
eISBN 978-0-7814-1088-5

The Team: Alex Field, Amy Konyndyk, Caitlyn Carlson, Karen Athen
Cover Design: Nick Lee

Printed in the United States of America

First Edition 2013

1 2 3 4 5 6 7 8 9 10

062113

To Audrey, Reid, and Norah. My prayer is that by the grace of God you might see that He is life and there is nothing to fear in death.

CONTENTS

INTRODUCTION

Our house is a lot of fun these days. Audrey is ten, Reid is seven, and little Norah is four. It's busy and can be a bit chaotic, but our home, by God's grace, is mostly filled with laughter (and occasionally the tears that follow discipline). Like most parents with children my kids' age, I am almost daily freaked out by how big they are getting. Gone are the days of changing diapers and burping babies after they eat. Compared to what they once were, all three of my kids look like Olympic athletes. There is no comparison between newborn Audrey and ten-year-old Audrey. She's almost a completely different person. She runs, rides her bike, roughhouses with her brother, and loves to have her girlfriends come over to play. I sometimes feel sad about how big she's grown, but the alternative would be something much more serious and scary.

What if she didn't grow up at all?

What if, instead of maturing and growing, she just stopped or reverted? What if as she turned two she still couldn't walk or talk? What if by age eight she couldn't read or dress herself? What if at ten she still needed me to carry her around and wipe the milk off her mouth?

Now don't get me wrong—if those things were necessary, I would gladly serve her and God in this way. But isn't this immeasurably more heartbreaking a thought than me not being able to hold her like an infant or enjoy her saying "hostible" instead of "hospital"? God created her to physically, emotionally, and mentally mature, and by His grace she has done just that! Our other two children are doing the same: *growing*. There are some parallels here to what we read about ourselves in Scripture. The Bible calls us to pursue maturity in Christ.

Consider just a few verses:

> Therefore let us leave the elementary doctrine of Christ and go on to maturity, not laying again a foundation of repentance from dead works and of faith toward God. (Heb. 6:1)

> Brothers, do not be children in your thinking. Be infants in evil, but in your thinking be mature. (1 Cor. 14:20)

> Him we proclaim, warning everyone and teaching everyone with all wisdom, that we

may present everyone mature in Christ. (Col. 1:28)

But solid food is for the mature, for those who have their powers of discernment trained by constant practice to distinguish good from evil. (Heb. 5:14)

I could go on, but I think the picture is clear. God wants us to grow from being infants in Christ to being mature in Christ. That's what this book is about. How are we to mature, and how can we spot any "developmental delays"? My prayer is that as you read this book, prayerfully applying its challenges to your heart, God would use Paul's letter to the Philippians to show you what maturity looks like and to call you to pursue it all the more with all your might under His grace.

CHAPTER ONE

ODD BEGINNINGS

I thank my God in all my remembrance of you. (Phil. 1:3)

The gospel absolutely *drove* Paul.

A missionary church planter, Paul's primary field of ministry was major metropolitan areas. If Paul were around today, he would be going to places like New York, Los Angeles, Dallas, and Chicago, and he would be planting churches. After developing a community of believers in these places, establishing leaders, and grounding them in the gospel, he would then move on to begin the work again in another area. But, a good shepherd, Paul tried to stay in contact with the churches he had planted. The churches would write to him with questions they had or about difficulties they faced, and Paul would write back with instruction and encouragement. The New Testament book we call Philippians is one of these encouraging missives, but it's fairly unique among Paul's letters.

Philippians is the only letter that we have in the Scriptures in which Paul is not trying to correct bad teaching or rebuke bad behavior. Instead, the letter highlights Paul's personal affection for the Philippian church and his commendation of (and exhortation toward) their Christian maturity. We see in this little letter what it looks like to be a mature man or woman in Jesus Christ.

Maybe you've already realized that Philippians is filled with what we might call "coffee-cup verses"—passages of Scripture that have so stirred the hearts and minds of believers over the years that we've thrown them on coffee cups, T-shirts, and bumper stickers. As a quick survey, we see in Philippians 1 that "to live is Christ, and to die is gain" (v. 21). In chapter 2 we get the famous proclamation of Jesus's sacrificial and humble self-emptying, learning that this humility makes Him worthy of all honor and glory but led Him to lay all of that aside to exalt God in service to sinners. In the third chapter, Paul says that he counts all things—even *good* things—as rubbish compared to the surpassing greatness of knowing Jesus Christ. And finally, in the fourth chapter, we find the epic and well-known declaration, "I can do all things through him who strengthens me" (v. 13).

Clearly, Paul has a lot to teach us about life—by which I mean he has a lot to teach us about Jesus.

If you read any of Paul's *other* letters, you will always find him saying, "Do this, don't do that, stop this, start doing that, quit going there, now act like this, get right, act right, be right." He grounds these commands in the finished work of Christ in the gospel, but they're still there. Paul apparently feels that these other churches have a lot of work to do. But Philippians is different. Paul gives the Philippians some instructions, sure, and he appears to address some issues needing correction, but he does so implicitly. Overall, the letter to the Philippians is colored with favor. It may be, then, that this letter is the best New Testament picture we have of what a maturing church looks like and what maturing people do.

As a result, the letter to the Philippians overflows with Paul's heart of affection for them. He considers the Philippians not just sheep in his care but friends in his heart, and in this book he wears his heart on his sleeve. You can glimpse the depth of his love for these people in his introductory remarks:

> Paul and Timothy, servants of Christ Jesus,
>
> To all the saints in Christ Jesus who are at Philippi, with the overseers and deacons:
>
> Grace to you and peace from God our Father and the Lord Jesus Christ.
>
> I thank my God in all my remembrance of you, always in every prayer of mine for you all making my prayer with joy, because of your partnership in the gospel from the first day until now. And I am sure of this, that he who began a good work in you will bring it to completion at the day of Jesus Christ. It is right for me to feel this way about you all, because I hold you in my heart, for you are all partakers with me of grace,

> both in my imprisonment and in the defense and
> confirmation of the gospel. For God is my wit-
> ness, how I yearn for you all with the affection of
> Christ Jesus. (1:1–8)

That last sentence may give the more stoic among us a bit of concern: "I yearn for you all with the affection of Christ Jesus." Of course, from what we know of Paul, he's a pretty tough guy. A man's man, perhaps. But he is moved enough by his connections with these friends of his to say that he "yearns" to be with them again, and this yearning is characterized by deep affection. *How deep is his affection?* It is affection sourced in the Lord Jesus Christ Himself.

This is the affection that took Jesus Christ to the cross. It is the affection that led Jesus to submit to arrest, to torture, to death. This is obviously a deep and abiding affection. And Paul is telling his friends that *all* this affection that is in Christ Jesus is in his own heart, which yearns for them.

Now, Paul loves all the churches to which he has written. He loves them all with the love of the Lord, and he has different kinds of connections to each one, which elicit varying degrees of personal affection. Remember in Galatians, for instance, how exasperated and angry he is. That's an expression of love as well, because he loves them enough to correct the church's acceptance of heresy. It's a loving shepherd who disciplines the sheep. In Ephesians, Paul reminds the Ephesian church that they were predestined before the foundation of the world. He tells them about God's feelings for them and about God's love for them. But he doesn't say, "I yearn for you." You are not going to find that language in Paul's letters to the other churches. You will find him often referencing who they are in Christ and what Christ did for them. He wishes them well, and he expresses love to them. But not like this. There is a serious affection here.

How did he get to feel this way about these people?

THE BLESSED BACKSTORY

Philippi was what we might call a major metropolitan area. Located along a major commercial road for the Roman Empire, the city teemed with industry and intelligentsia, agriculturalists and artists. Since it was a well-populated city with lots going on, it made sense that a missionary church planter like Paul would want to go there and preach the gospel. So to get a fuller picture of the affectionate connection revealed in his letter to the Philippians, we need to look further back at the roots of his relationships there. We will start in Acts 16.

> So, setting sail from Troas, we made a direct voyage to Samothrace, and the following day to Neapolis, and from there to Philippi, which is a leading city of the district of Macedonia and a Roman colony. We remained in this city some days. And on the Sabbath day we went outside the gate to the riverside, where we supposed there

was a place of prayer, and we sat down and spoke
to the women who had come together. One who
heard us was a woman named Lydia, from the
city of Thyatira, a seller of purple goods, who was
a worshiper of God. The Lord opened her heart
to pay attention to what was said by Paul. And
after she was baptized, and her household as well,
she urged us, saying, "If you have judged me to
be faithful to the Lord, come to my house and
stay." And she prevailed upon us. (vv. 11–15)

Previously, Paul received a vision in which he saw a Macedonian
man calling for help, which Paul took as a spiritual calling. Without
delay, he and three companions—Luke, Silas, and Paul's young
protégé, Timothy—set off for Macedonia, which brought them
to Philippi.

The fact that the group is looking for a synagogue but finds
instead what is basically a women's Bible study shows not only
the lack of Christian presence in Philippi but the lack of Jewish
presence. Typically Paul and his cohorts sought out a Jewish house
of worship in which to proclaim the good news of the Messiah,
Jesus Christ, but Philippi was such a densely Roman city that
there were not even enough Jewish males to constitute a place of
worship. Instead, where the missionaries expect to find a "place
of prayer," they come upon a group of religious women having
their own riverside Sabbath service. This is where Paul first meets
Lydia.

THE BUSINESSWOMAN

Lydia is from the city of Thyatira. This tells us that she is likely ethnically Asian. But she has a house in Philippi. So this tells us that economically she's very wealthy. Both Thyatira and Philippi are major metropolitan areas. The portrait we see developing of Lydia is that of a woman who's in the fashion industry—think "fashionista"—essentially the CEO of her own fashion empire. Thinking in today's terms, she'd have a house in Los Angeles, a house in New York, and a house in Paris. This is a woman who has done very, very well for herself.

But Lydia is also what the Bible calls a God-fearer. Here's what that means: She has rejected paganism. She has rejected polytheism. She does not believe that there are dozens of gods—that there's a god of the wind, a god of the rain, a god of the purple cloth, or a god of the fashion world. She's worshipping the Father, not Prada. Lydia has come to believe that there is one God. She listens to the teaching of the Jews, trying to grasp what it means to live a God-fearing life; she wants to live out her faith in the context of her family and her business.

This is an important point in the story of Lydia's conversion: she is an intellect and, by all indications, *a seeker*. She has gathered with a group of women to hear the Scriptures explained. Lydia, by listening to the Torah, knows that God gave His people the law. She knows that God gave the Ten Commandments. She understands that she does some of those things well, but she also understands that she's broken some of those laws and commandments too. She likely has some concept of the need for atonement. But without the good news of Jesus, she's confused. It is into this setting that Paul shows up and starts to fill in the spiritual framework through which Lydia has operated up to this point.

This is like a Tuesday-morning women's Bible study! This is like a bunch of women doing a Hebrew precepts study, and Paul shows up, says, "Hold on a second," and presses pause. Paul begins to explain to the women's Bible study that God gave us the law to reveal that we all have fallen short of God's glory and that atonement was made only by Christ's work on the cross.

Paul engages Lydia's reason, engages her intellect—and it is through the impartation of this knowledge that she becomes a believer in Christ. In fact, she immediately believes and gets baptized, her whole household gets saved and baptized, and then she invites Paul to stay in her home. I'm guessing she's got a nice joint. For Paul the bi-vocational missionary and blue-collar tent maker, this is a pretty sweet deal. His time in Philippi is a refreshing respite from the glorious grind of faithfulness to the gospel call.

THE SLAVE GIRL

This is how the church in Philippi began: the conversion of the high-society businesswoman Lydia through intellectual engagement with the gospel. But the story, like the church, becomes more complex. As Acts 16 continues, we see how the mission in Philippi reveals the diversity of the church being planted there:

As we were going to the place of prayer, we were met by a slave girl who had a spirit of divination and brought her owners much gain by fortune-telling. She followed Paul and us, crying out, "These men are servants of the Most High God, who proclaim to you the way of salvation." And this she kept doing for many days. Paul, having become greatly annoyed, turned and said to the spirit, "I command you in the name of Jesus Christ to come out of her." And it came out that very hour. But when her owners saw that their hope of gain was gone, they seized Paul and Silas and dragged them into the marketplace before the rulers. (vv. 16–19)

This little girl stands in absolute contrast to Lydia. Where Lydia is Asian, this girl is Greek. Where Lydia is in control, an intellect, this little girl is impoverished, enslaved, and exploited. Where Lydia is a seeker, this little girl proclaims the way of salvation. Of course, she's doing it perhaps unwittingly, under demonic control, but she believes that salvation is available the same way the demons do. While Paul and Lydia meet in the context of a formal, orderly group meeting, Paul and the slave girl meet as she follows the missionaries around, screaming her head off. She is disruptive. As in control as Lydia is, this little girl is out of control.

Now watch how God goes after her. Paul doesn't turn around and say, "I'm doing a seminar Saturday on 'Crazy.' I would like for you to come because I think you have crazy in you." He does not invite her to a Bible study, and he does not appeal to her intellect on any level. He doesn't appeal to her reason. She's irrational. No—instead, in an act of Holy Spirit power, he rebukes and exorcises the spirit that rules her and enslaves her on the inside. In an instant she finds the salvation she's been demonically mocking.

The contrast between these two Philippian conversions is startling and instructive. With Lydia, the gospel gets at her heart when Paul engages her *intellectually*. With the slave girl, the gospel gets at her heart when Paul engages her *spiritually*. In both instances, the Holy Spirit grants new birth and repentance, of course, but the deliverance of the gospel takes on the context of the personal need. Paul shows how he as a missionary is willing to become all things to all people (1 Cor. 9:22).

But the conversions aren't done.

THE BLUE-COLLAR JOE

The deliverance and conversion of the possessed slave girl is an exciting scene, but the story intensifies as we continue reading in Acts 16:

> And when they had brought them to the magistrates, they said, "These men are Jews, and they are disturbing our city. They advocate customs that are not lawful for us as Romans to accept or practice." The crowd joined in attacking them, and the magistrates tore the garments off them

and gave orders to beat them with rods. And
when they had inflicted many blows upon them,
they threw them into prison, ordering the jailer
to keep them safely. Having received this order,
he put them into the inner prison and fastened
their feet in the stocks. (vv. 20–24)

As Westerners, when we think of "the stocks," we picture New
England in the 1700s, the embarrassment and shame of having your
head and hands stuck in a public contraption. But that is not what
first-century Roman Empire stocks were like. These devious contrap-
tions would contort the prisoner's body into all sorts of excruciating
postures, locking limbs and joints in place to the point of making the
entire body cramp. The prisoner's body would seize up with searing
pain, and then the Romans would just leave the person there for days.

Notice that the jailer is not commanded to treat his prisoners
this way. The magistrates simply ask him to keep the missionaries
safe, and instead he tortures them. So we aren't dealing with a very
nice man at this moment. This jailer is very good at his job, and he
probably likes it more than he should.

But when it comes to taking pride in one's work, this guy
could not out-enjoy Paul. "About midnight Paul and Silas were
praying and singing hymns to God, and the prisoners were listening to them" (Acts 16:25). If you hated the gospel, wouldn't the
apostle Paul be the most frustrating human being alive? It did not
matter what anyone did to this man, he loved God and continued
to show it in every possible way.

We see Paul's gospel fixation echoed throughout his letter to the Philippians. He is the man who when threatened says, "Well, to die is gain." In response his captors will say, "We'll torture you, then." He says, "I don't count the present suffering as worthy to even compare to the future glory." You can't win with a guy like this. If you want to kill him, he's cool with that because it means he gets to be with Jesus. If you want to make him suffer, he's cool with that, so long as it makes him like Jesus. If you want to let him live, he's fine with that, because to him, "to live is Christ." Paul is, as Richard Sibbes says of everyone united with Christ, a man who "can never be conquered."[1]

Paul's stubborn fixation on Jesus is reminiscent of these words from the early church father John Chrysostom, who apparently was threatened with banishment if he did not renounce his faith:

> If the empress wishes to banish me, let her do so;
> "the earth is the Lord's." If she wants to have me
> sawn asunder, I will have Isaiah for an example.
> If she wants me to be drowned in the ocean, I
> think of Jonah. If I am to be thrown in the fire,
> the three men in the furnace suffered the same.
> If cast before wild beasts, I remember Daniel
> in the lion's den. If she wants me to be stoned,
> I have before me Stephen, the first martyr. If
> she demands my head, let her do so; John the
> Baptist shines before me. Naked I came from my
> mother's womb, naked shall I leave this world.

Paul reminds me, "If I still pleased men, I would not be the servant of Christ."[2]

Sounds a lot like Paul, doesn't it? In response to his bold missionary work in a hostile place, the Romans put him in the inner prison and lock him in the stocks, and he basically says, "I'm going to sing and pray while I'm down here."

And as he and Silas are singing and praying, something extraordinary happens.

> Suddenly there was a great earthquake, so that the foundations of the prison were shaken. And immediately all the doors were opened, and everyone's bonds were unfastened. When the jailer woke and saw that the prison doors were open, he drew his sword and was about to kill himself, supposing that the prisoners had escaped. But Paul cried with a loud voice, "Do not harm yourself, for we are all here." And the jailer called for lights and rushed in, and trembling with fear he fell down before Paul and Silas. Then he brought them out and said, "Sirs, what must I do to be saved?" And they said, "Believe in the Lord Jesus, and you will be saved, you and your household." And they spoke the word of the Lord to him and to all who were in his house. And he took them the same hour of the night

and washed their wounds; and he was baptized at
once, he and all his family. Then he brought them
up into his house and set food before them. And
he rejoiced along with his entire household that
he had believed in God. (Acts 16:26–34)

This is one more utterly unique conversion story to help us
develop a portrait of the Philippian church. The jailer is not like our
first two character studies. The jailer is basically a blue-collar ex-GI
manning the jail cells. He is not interested in the incessant banter of
the intellectuals, and he's not invested in the charismatic hoopla of
spiritual power. He is like the guy who just wants to put in his time
at work so he can go home, have a beer, and watch the game. He is
probably not a guy who sits around a lot thinking about the mean-
ing of life. He's duty bound. He just wants to do his job well, honor
his imperial employers, and get back to his well-ordered house. On
the scale of Lydia to the slave girl, the jailer is middle class. Not super
rich and not poor.

How does the gospel grab hold of him?

In Rome during this period of time, if a prisoner escaped or was
lost, whoever was responsible for that prisoner would pay the price
with his life. Like a lot of blue-collar Joes of today, this jailer has
come to identify his life with his job. There are people today who
cannot think of themselves except by what they do, and perhaps
this man is no different. So when he sees that he might be about
to lose a lot of what has been entrusted to him, it's an automatic
leap for him to think of taking his own life. He immediately yanks

out his sword and gets ready to kill himself. But Paul shows him a better identity, a more fulfilling reality, and a greater duty that transcends everything this guy has previously known.

He shows the jailer this reality first by example. After being tortured, the missionaries sing and pray. After becoming free from their bonds, even though the opportunity for escape and revenge is before them, the missionaries stay to share the gospel. When they have the chance to run away, they stay. And the jailer is blown away. While Paul engaged Lydia through her intellect and the slave girl through spiritual power, he engages the jailer through a living witness to a miracle.

This is how the Philippian church begins—with a Jewish fashionista businesswoman, a demon-possessed slave girl, and a blue-collar ex-GI duty bound to the Roman Empire. Probably not exactly your dream church-planting team, but the Spirit works in strange ways to utterly redeem the unlikeliest and most diverse people. We see in the backstory of Acts 16 the beautiful reconciliation that the gospel achieves, not just of unholy individuals to a holy God but superficially incompatible people to each other! Jesus takes strangers and makes them a family.

THE GOSPEL'S NEW COMMUNITY

Now we see that when Paul writes to the Philippians, "I yearn for you all with the affection of Christ Jesus," it's because he was *there*. He's talking about Lydia. He's talking about this little slave girl.

He's talking about the jailer. When he says, "I thank God in all my remembrance of you," these are the people he remembers.

By the time Paul writes to the Philippians, how old is the little girl? What sort of young woman has she grown up to be? It's been roughly ten to fifteen years since the planting of the Philippian church. Is the young girl married? Does she have children? What about Lydia? What has Lydia done for the good of the gospel with all her wealth? What about the jailer—has he softened, or is he still rough around the edges?

Paul knows this church. He has won the souls of this church. He baptized them. He was the conduit through which the power of the Holy Spirit poured out. This is why he's yearning for them with the affection of Jesus Christ.

It is from his experience with the Philippians and other missionary journeys—stemming from his own stunning conversion from Jewish persecutor of the church to proclaimer of Jesus Christ to the Gentiles—that Paul has adopted the position that the gospel cannot be stopped by the socioeconomic, racial, or religious walls we fallen humans build up. In these incredible instances, the gospel defies race, defies class, defies status, and even defies aptitude.

If we're honest with ourselves, we will admit that we tend to prefer to do life with people who are similar to us. We live in neighborhoods and associate with people who look like us and act like us. Most of us go to church with people similar to us. This is the natural tendency of all people. *But the gospel is not natural.* As we see here in the odd beginnings of the Philippian church, the gospel blows the doors off our tidy little hegemonic communes and creates a whole new community that never would have formed without it. Apart from the supernaturally reconciling ministry of grace, rich fashionistas are not doing life with poor demoniacs. It just isn't happening. But because Paul is willing to put skin in the game, risking his own life to bring the message of life in Christ, what was once divided is now unified in love.

This is the kind of thing that emboldens Paul. This supernatural community makes him bolder in ministry because it gives him a clearer picture of the gospel's effects among people. He really sees the gospel going forth into the world, bearing fruit, and growing (Col. 1:6). And it bears fruit within people too, not just among them.

The gospel creates a new reality that deepens our understanding of the world and our place in it. This is where Paul is going in the book of Philippians. As he remembers the powerful conversions he's witnessed, he wants to bring to their minds the soul-strengthening assurance of life in Christ day-to-day, wherever they may find themselves—rich or poor, healthy or sick, alive or dead. And he isn't just blowing smoke here. As the roots of the Philippian church plant reach to Paul's time in prison, his affectionate remembrance in the letter comes from a prison too. You see, Paul wrote to his friends in Philippi from a jail cell.

CHAPTER TWO

THE WORTHY LIFE

*Only let your manner of life be worthy of
the gospel of Christ. (Phil. 1:27)*

Through the gospel, Jesus is making a people for Himself. We call this people the church, and it is made up of individuals from every tongue, tribe, race, and nation. The new covenant creates a new community—one that brings Jew and Gentile, male and female, slave and free all together—and makes a new humanity out of them as they are united in Christ by faith in Christ. But the gospel doesn't just transcend and transform our human institutions and divisions; it also transcends and transforms our circumstances.

After Paul greets the Philippians with personal and pastoral affection, he continues his letter by highlighting the ongoing, in-the-moment power of the good news.

> I want you to know, brothers, that what has
> happened to me has really served to advance
> the gospel, so that it has become known
> throughout the whole imperial guard and to
> all the rest that my imprisonment is for Christ.
> (Phil. 1:12–13)

Paul is in prison. Again. Each time, he is not sure if he will be released or executed. And even when he is free from prison, he is not free from threats to his life. But notice his perspective on the entire situation. He can see his troubles and imprisonment only through the lens of grace-fueled optimism. The gospel has become known throughout the imperial guard! Wouldn't it make sense that seeing conversions among his current captors would make Paul remember the conversion of the Philippian jailer? Wouldn't these unlikely responses to Jesus Christ remind him of the way Lydia and the slave girl had come to Christ?

The gospel not only begins to spread throughout the imperial guard, but others are encouraged to boldly proclaim the gospel all the more: "And most of the brothers, having become confident in the Lord by my imprisonment, are much more bold to speak the word without fear" (Phil. 1:14). It is astounding to consider the level at which Paul regards his life as a sacrifice. He sees his imprisonment as the sacrifice necessary to make the rest of the brothers bold, fearless sharers of the gospel. He sees his trials as the sacrifices necessary to win the lost to Christ. If it means death, he will be willing to go there to bring others home.

For the cause of Christ, Paul appears ready and willing to trade in things many of us hold sacred every day—namely, our sense of justice and security. We can see this clearly in what he says next:

> Some indeed preach Christ from envy and rivalry, but others from good will. The latter do it out of love, knowing that I am put here for the defense of the gospel. The former proclaim Christ out of selfish ambition, not sincerely but thinking to afflict me in my imprisonment. What then? Only that in every way, whether in pretense or in truth, Christ is proclaimed, and in that I rejoice. (Phil. 1:15–18)

What is happening here? Well, when you take a dominant leader like Paul and remove him from the scene, other ambitious people start filling in the gap. Nature, as they say, abhors a vacuum—and so it goes if you remove strong leadership. When Alexander the Great died, for example, his whole empire began to crumble within three to five years. *Why?* Because the void he left began to fill up with warring factions jockeying for power. A similar thing is happening in Paul's absence. When he is imprisoned, others seek to fill his position. Some, as he says, preach Christ, but they have no intention of trying to fill Paul's shoes. They do not preach out of love, out of "good will," or to continue the ministry of what made Paul *Paul*, which was actually not Paul himself but Christ. Rather, others try to usurp the mantle of leadership out of "selfish ambition," seeking Paul's position to steal glory from him and ultimately from God. But Paul has a remarkable perspective on even this wicked self-interest. "If Christ is proclaimed," he reasons, "in that I will rejoice" (Phil. 1:18, author's translation).

Is it any wonder that this sentiment comes from the heart of a man who has seen Christ save through intellect, through power, and through example? He has seen Christ save in even the darkest circumstances of persecution and prison. Paul knows that God will make His name known and that God can use our evil for His good. From Paul's perspective, in the light of the gospel, everything must serve the purpose of the glory of Christ, so it isn't therefore a tragedy that Paul's in prison being persecuted within or unjustly maligned without. No, it is a privilege. Paul considers it a blessing to be considered worthy to suffer for the cause of Christ. This is not the kind of Christianity any of us end up with except through a profound experiencing of Christ's cross applied to our lives.

WORTH LIVING FOR

Paul uses the word *worthy* several times in his letters to the churches. In Ephesians 4:1, he writes about walking in a way that is worthy of God's call. In Colossians 1:10, he writes about walking in a manner worthy of the Lord. In 1 Thessalonians 2:12, he writes about walking in a manner worthy of God. In 2 Thessalonians 1:5, he urges living in a way worthy of the kingdom of God.

What does this word *worthy* mean?

For Paul, it means *ascribing worth*. When he commands others to live in a "worthy" way, he means we should live in such a way that shows what we believe is of supreme worth. For Christians, it means living in such a way that Jesus is seen as big, that Jesus is seen as glorious.

See, in the spiritual economy of Paul, God and His gospel are most important, not Paul and his well-being. Christ has so captivated Paul that Christ has become all to him. So when people preach Christ, whether in pretense or in truth, Paul rejoices that Christ is proclaimed. Though some mean to harm Paul, he considers his harm a fair trade for the opportunity to proclaim Jesus. It is this spiritual stability, born of a gospel-focused heart, that gives Paul peace and contentment—and yes, *joy*—no matter where he finds himself.

"In prison," he says, "I'll rejoice. Living at Lydia's house, I'll rejoice. Either way, I'll rejoice."

> Yes, and I will rejoice, for I know that through your prayers and the help of the Spirit of Jesus Christ this will turn out for my deliverance, as it is my eager expectation and hope that I will not be at all ashamed, but that with full courage now as always Christ will be honored in my body, whether by life or by death. For to me to live is Christ. (Phil. 1:18–21)

Well, of course! Of course it is. It's easy to confess that living is Christ, isn't it? *Not so fast.* The confession and the conviction don't always go together. Paul's confession erupts from deep conviction. He's seen that living could be nothing else but Christ. He's seen it in his ministry over and over again.

Lydia has everything. She has everything any of us could ever want. She's wealthy, intelligent, powerful. She's got those things most of us spend up our lives to get. But where would she end up without Christ? Spiritually bankrupt. All of her treasures come with expiration dates. Would Paul live for that?

The little girl who let the bitterness and anger at being sold into slavery corrode her soul to the point of vulnerability to demonic oppression? Is that a fair life option for Paul? He's certainly been betrayed and assaulted and thrown into captivity. He is no stranger to the temptation of vengeance.

Lydia, the slave girl, and the jailer—they were all slaves in their own ways to the kind of lives men and women choose all the time, and Paul saw the moral brokenness and spiritual dysfunction of it all. He also saw the joy that comes when the gospel heals, transforms, and restores. Paul himself once lived out of bitterness and malice, persecuting the church he later came to love. Then God hijacked his life. The zealous Pharisee became the apostle with the gospeled heart.

So of course he would say, "To live is Christ." In the logic of the gospel, there are no alternatives to Christ. Every other option is no option at all. When everything considered valuable in life is seen to be nothing in comparison to the glory of Christ, you learn rather well that Christ alone is worth living for. Christ alone is worthy of an entire life's affections and devotions. He is worthy of so much more, in fact, which is why Paul completes his declaration "to live is Christ" this way: "to die is gain."

WORTH DYING FOR

"For to me to live is Christ, and to die is gain" (Phil. 1:21). Hemmed in on all sides by the grace of God, being placed in Christ and having Christ living in him, Paul knows he is covered not just in life but in death as well. When God promises life to those who trust Him, He gives *eternal* life.

> If I am to live in the flesh, that means fruitful labor for me. Yet which I shall choose I cannot tell. I am hard pressed between the two. My desire is to depart and be with Christ, for that is far better. But to remain in the flesh is more necessary on your account. Convinced of this, I know that I will remain and continue with you all, for your progress and joy in the faith, so that in me you may have ample cause to glory in Christ Jesus, because of my coming to you again. (Phil. 1:22–26)

Elsewhere Paul says, "If in Christ we have hope in this life only, we are of all people most to be pitied" (1 Cor. 15:19). There is a greater day coming, a greater reward coming, a greater life coming, and the purpose of life while we are alive is to walk in a manner worthy of the gospel, which holds the promise of life everlasting.

Jesus says, "Even if you die, you will live" (John 11:25, author's translation). For those united to Christ by faith, death has no sting and no victory (1 Cor. 15:55). In fact, to be present with the Lord is better than life! The great preacher Dwight Moody once quipped, "Some day you will read in the papers that D. L. Moody, of East Northfield, is dead. Don't you believe a word of it! At that moment I shall be more alive than I am now."[1]

Death is a homecoming for the Christian. Paul sees it as gain because he sees it as the reward for offering himself as a living sacrifice on this side of the veil. So in prison, Paul is saying, "It would be better to go home." And in the comfort and opulence of Lydia's house, he's saying, "It would be better to go home."

MAKING THE GOSPEL LOOK BIG

Paul loves the Philippian church so much, he begins to plead with them to want something better than any other thing they could want: "Only let your manner of life be worthy of the gospel of Christ" (Phil. 1:27).

By itself, that is a daunting challenge. Is it even possible to live in a way that is worthy of the gospel? Isn't the gospel—*because it brings us eternal life in Jesus*—of infinite worth? I don't know about you, but this calling feels impossible to me.

Thankfully, Paul does not leave us with an ambiguous command. He continues:

Only let your manner of life be worthy of the gospel of Christ, so that whether I come and see you or am absent, I may hear of you that you are standing firm in one spirit. (Phil. 1:27)

The apostle once again links the gospel's power to that eclectic, strange group of humanity assembled by the Holy Spirit into a new community called the body of Christ. The wealthy business-woman, the poor slave girl, and the blue-collar Joe stand together as a testimony to the power of the gospel in Philippi. What does it look like to live life in a manner worthy of the gospel? It looks like dying with Christ to one's self and being raised in Christ to walk in the newness of life with our brothers and sisters. It means living grace-filled lives that grant patience and mercy and gentleness for the spiritual journeys of others and a respect for the differences and idiosyncrasies we all bring to the Lord's table.

The ground is level at the foot of Christ's cross.

This is not an easy walk in our consumer culture in which everything is so polarized. From religion to politics to pop culture, everybody believes that their way is *the* way. We treat our celebrities like idols and our politicians like messiahs. Within the church, we treat our ministries and church-growth models as inviolable laws of nature. We start thinking that our way of doing church is the only way of doing church. We believe that our way of preaching is the only way to preach. In these wild swings of the ideological pen-dulum, we go well beyond what the Scriptures actually command. And the result is a monochromatic, one-dimensional church and an impotent "gospel." In this disunity there is a fundamental denial of the power of Jesus Christ to make the Spanish-speaking day laborer my brother, an Asian woman selling clothes my sister, a house church in the Brazilian slums my family. When all of us, different kinds of people, walk together in unity for the glory of Christ, the gospel looks really big.

The gospel of Jesus Christ is worth living for, *yes*, and it is worth dying for, *of course*, but we show it is supremely valuable to us when we deny ourselves and take up our crosses to be a blessing to the people who the gospel is calling us to. No more ideological pendulum swings. No more being swayed by every wind of false doctrine. No more being moved to and fro by speculations and myths and doubts and self-interest. Instead, we (together) stand "firm in one spirit" (Phil. 1:27).

When we forego our own way to stand together in the spirit of Christ, we make the gospel look supremely valuable. And now that we've removed our energy and affections from selfish ambitions, we can move out on mission together, "with one mind striving side by side for the faith of the gospel" (Phil. 1:27).

Let me tell you the wrong way to read these stories. I think that sometimes we read the Bible and think everybody we read about is different from us. I think we believe that Lydia got converted and never wrestled with doubt or fear again. We think that the slave girl came to know Christ and never struggled with her bitterness, anger, or ability to forgive again. We think that the duty-bound jailer converted and then immediately became so filled with the Holy Spirit that he floated around in Shekinah glory, converting the rest of the Roman legion there in Philippi. But it's not true. Paul says to the Philippians that to live a life worthy of the gospel means standing together as one, striving in one mind for what's ahead. Implicitly, we see that the Philippian church was not a perfect church; in fact, the gospel is commended when we can admit we aren't perfect, even after we're saved.

This is purely speculation, but do you suppose there is a chance that as the church at Philippi grew, Lydia starts to stuggle with pride? She's got a big house. She funds a big part of what's going on in the church. There's a possibility that, over time, she could become quite the control freak. If you know the CEO type, maybe you see that it's possible she might think her ideas for how to do things in the church are the right ideas.

What about the slave girl? Do you suppose that, as she gets older, she might have some relationship issues? Do you think that perhaps she might struggle with trusting people, particularly men?

Do you think that our blue-collar ex-GI might need the Lord to soften his heart and warm him up a little bit? Maybe he struggles with being gruff and handling everyone like they've got the thick skin of a soldier or prisoner.

Maybe it's stuff like this that's behind Paul's encouragement in Philippians 1:6: "And I am sure of this, that he who began a good work in you will bring it to completion at the day of Jesus Christ."

Living a life worthy of the gospel does not mean pretending to be perfect. Instead, it means having the humility to think of others as better than ourselves (Phil. 2:3). It means putting self-concern aside to work together, realizing that we are all still in process. Let us have the grace of God for each other that He gave us in the overlooking of sins and the outpouring of unmerited love. And together we can strive in the holiness imputed to us in Christ and promised to us in the age to come.

GOSPEL COURAGE

We have seen so far that living a life worthy of the gospel means being humble and seeking unity. These are concepts Paul will continue to develop throughout this letter. But before Philippians 1 ends, he gives us another characteristic of the worthy life, something else that makes the gospel look big.

What does it look like to have a mature Christian life?

> Only let your manner of life be worthy of the gospel of Christ, so that whether I come and see you or am absent, I may hear of you that you are standing firm in one spirit, with one mind striving side by side for the faith of the gospel, and not frightened in anything by your opponents. (Phil. 1:27–28)

The Christian living a life worthy of the gospel of Jesus Christ is fearless, regardless of the situation.

I believe that this concept is difficult for us even though most of us are not going to find our lives in danger because of our faith. At this point in time, even as Christians become more and more marginalized in the wider culture, it's still highly unlikely that someone's going to plot to murder you or even become aggressively violent toward you simply because of your faith. But there are still plenty of ways that fear and courage apply to our context.

I have a dear friend who has a beautiful wife, one very precocious little girl, and one little boy who's the mellowest kid I've ever seen in my life. My friend loves his family very much. He makes a good living, lives in a great house, and has great friends. He enjoys a really good life. I think, regardless of where you come from, you could look at his life and think, *He's very blessed.*

My friend recently got on a plane to Darfur to go to one of the most dangerous places in the world to dig wells for people. He went to help provide clean drinking water for people he did not know and who, by and large, do not care for him. Some of them would rather he die than be there to give them clean drinking water. As he went, he was betting it all on the providence of God that he wouldn't run across the wrong crowd at the wrong time. Because if you do, out in the desert in some of the places his group had to travel, you are dead.

Now, why would he leave a beautiful wife and two awesome kids and get on a plane to go dig water wells for people who would just as soon kill him as drink his water? *Why would he do that?* Because to live is Christ and to die is gain.

From our Western comfort zone, that can be seen as an extreme example of gospel-fueled courage. But don't we need this sort of confidence in Christ to simply overcome the fear of sharing the gospel with our neighbors?

Paul talks about marginalization, insults, oppression, persecution, and suffering as if they're *gifts*. They are "granted" to us to further the cause of Christ, which is the goal we all strive toward together.

The day will come—*perhaps today*—when you will die and see all of history being effectively rewritten from the halls of heaven. The annals of history will not be filled with wars and kings; there will be one story, the heroes will be missionaries, and the victor will be seen clearly as Christ. Knowing this, who cares if friends or enemies mock you? Do not be "frightened in anything by your opponents" (Phil. 1:28). Be willing to get on a plane and go to dangerous places. Be willing to take the pay cut at work to do what's right. Be willing, no matter who your opponent is, to be fearless.

Why?

> This is a clear sign to them of their destruction, but of your salvation, and that from God. For it has been granted to you that for the sake of Christ you should not only believe in him but also suffer for his sake, engaged in the same conflict that you saw I had and now hear that I still have. (Phil. 1:28–30)

To be opposed because of our faith is a sign of our opponent's destruction. Ironic, isn't it? Especially given that it was the Christian's destruction the early church's persecutors had in mind.

In fact, to be opposed for our faith in Christ is a blessing because it is in itself a sign of our salvation! Jesus puts it this way:

> Blessed are those who are persecuted for righteousness' sake, for theirs is the kingdom of heaven.
>
> Blessed are you when others revile you and persecute you and utter all kinds of evil against you falsely on my account. Rejoice and be glad, for your reward is great in heaven, for so they persecuted the prophets who were before you. (Matt. 5:10–12)

Fearless faith results from holding on to Christ as our treasure. Gospel courage comes from gospel preciousness. If we truly believed that our reward in heaven far surpasses all the comfort and convenience and collections of the world, we, too, would be willing to consider them all as loss.

Paul encourages those in the Philippian church to remember the gospel that saved them, the gospel that brought them all together and made them family, the gospel that secures them second by second for the glorification of eternity so that they will hold all else loosely and ultimately fear nothing.

The wealthy businesswoman, the fortune-telling slave girl, the duty-bound jailer—they all found a greater thing, a more beautiful thing, a more glorious thing than what they'd been holding on to before. Liberated by Jesus and totally secured, they could lose all confidence in the flesh and find unassailable courage in their redeemer.

So what does it look like to live a life worthy of the gospel of Jesus Christ? It looks like walking with, loving with, and doing life with those who are different from you. What binds you together is Christ. It looks like striving together to make Christ known. What motivates you is Christ. And it looks like standing with courage against all oppressors, natural or supernatural. What secures you is Christ.

To live is Christ, and to die is gain.

Christ is all. Looking at it that way, the implication becomes rather simple. Not easy. But simple. If a mature Christian life, or a life worthy of the gospel of Jesus Christ, is a life where you are living deeply with others, regardless of external differences, if you strive for a deeper faith and grow in your faith together, pressing into Christ together, chasing Him together, and if it is fearlessness in faith … *how are you doing?*

Fearlessly face that question.

Are you living a life worthy of the gospel of Jesus Christ? Have you found Christ worth living for, worth dying for, worth casting all away for His sake? Examine your own heart. Do you just hang out with people who are like you? Are you timid and fearful when it comes to any opposition to your faith? In the end, are you growing in God, or are you stagnant and cold? Remember, we're talking about what it looks like to be maturing in Christ.

Face these questions with courage, and press on. Jesus loves you.

CHAPTER THREE

THE ONE GOD EXALTS

Do nothing from selfish ambition or conceit. (Phil. 2:3)

Philippians 2 is mean. I don't know how else to sum it up except that it's mean. This is what I mean by *mean*: Philippians 2 goes after the heart. There are parts of Philippians 1 that sort of lean on your heart and might even tug at your heart, but Philippians 2 violently goes after the heart of your faith. In the way of the Spirit, the passages here assault our pride and bind up our wounds with grace. Maybe you've heard that the preaching of the gospel afflicts the comfortable and comforts the afflicted. This is the dynamic in play in Philippians 2.

The motivation of this meanness—and of course I don't mean anger or malice, but more ferocity and fierceness—is the exaltation of the almighty God. Somewhat belied by the hymn of humility Paul shares with us in the opening lines of this chapter is the desire to create passionate worshippers of the God who is a consuming fire. The central idea of Philippians 2 is so abundant in the Scriptures that if you were to wring out the Bible, this is what you'd end up with: "The fear of the LORD is the beginning of wisdom" (Ps. 111:10; Prov. 9:10).

As we connect the conversions in the backstory of the Philippian church to the letter at hand, we ought to recall the sort of fear of God that drives sinners into His loving arms. Most people coming to Christ fear hell and punishment for their sins. That's a completely rational fear to have once you know the facts. And it's a good fear. But it's not the best fear to have in that moment of conversion, mainly because it cannot sustain the Christian life. We are not called by a spirit of fear into a spirit of fear but by the Spirit of grace into a spirit of love and power.

This fear we ought to have of God is not so much terror as it is *awe*.

Our church does a family camp every summer where we go out in the woods. There's a little petting zoo at this camp for the children, and inside that petting zoo they have fainting goats. I kid you not. They have goats. That faint. YouTube it; it's a real thing, and it's fantastic.

If you sneak up on these goats and startle them, their legs will lock up, they will black out, and they will fall over. On the first day of camp, the directors give us the tour, and we walk into the pen with the fainting goats, and the directors plainly say, "Please don't jack with the goats." And of course every man in the group is thinking, *That goat will faint if I jack with it? All right.* And they immediately start thinking of creative ways to get the goats to faint, trying to see how quickly they can make the goat lock up and black out. They'll suddenly shout, "Ah!" or smack it on the bottom, whatever works. It becomes a contest to see who can make the goat faint fastest.

Now, let me propose that this game would look totally different if instead of a goat in the pen there was a lion. If there was a lion in the pen, I don't think anybody would run in shouting at it or smacking it on the butt. Maybe if a lion was in a petting zoo, some might think it was safe enough to go in and pet it or just hang out quietly. Maybe. But no sane person is making a ruckus in a pen with a lion. Nobody's playing the game "Let's Startle the Apex Predator." Instead, there is respect. There is a knowing of our place. *That's a lion. I'm a man. He could eat me.* This inspires fear. This inspires awe. That's the kind of healthy fear we ought to have of God. He's like Narnia's Aslan—we know He's good, but He's not safe.

The kind of fear that the early Philippian converts knew was the biblical "fear of God." This is the kind of fear that typifies the work of sanctification (Phil. 2:12). It is the reverent, humble, awed kind of fear. Don't you think the slave girl and the jailer especially knew this kind of fear? Their conversion experiences presented stark evidence of God's power over the forces of nature and the satanic realm. Paul's own conversion experience was one of vivid Christological manifestation; surely his extraordinary conversion translated to his extraordinary ministry.

It is this kind of worshipful, put-in-our-place, awed fear that colors Paul's words in Philippians 2.

GODLY FEAR HUMBLES

Paul begins this section of his address with these words: "So if there is any encouragement in Christ …" (Phil. 2:1). He does not mean this as speculatively as it sounds. He is not trying to imply that there may not be any encouragement in Christ. He is only saying, "If you grant the premise that there is encouragement in Christ," knowing his recipients, with as much as they've been through in their lives, know from experience that there is *much* encouragement to be had in Christ.

What is the encouragement?

First, it is that all can be saved regardless of background, aptitude, sin, or family history. When we are saved, we are saved by grace, and grace implies "in spite of." We are saved in spite of so much! That is great encouragement.

Paul continues:

> So if there is any encouragement in Christ, any
> comfort from love, any participation in the Spirit,
> any affection and sympathy, complete my joy by
> being of the same mind, having the same love,
> being in full accord and of one mind. (Phil. 2:1–2)

Is there comfort from love? Absolutely! And there is eternal comfort from the love of God. Paul is helping the Philippians connect the dots between what they've received and what they owe. In Romans 13:8, Paul writes, "Owe no one anything, except to love each other." That is the shorthand version of what he's saying here in Philippians 2. If you're encouraged by Christ's salvation, if you've received any comfort from the Father's love, if the Spirit's empowering presence dwells in you, go all the way in the Christian experience—this is what he's urging them to do when he says "complete my joy"—by living in unity with each other, loving each other, and working together to exalt Christ.

In this, Paul echoes the gist of Philippians 1. In other words, he is saying here what he also says there: if the gospel is true, your life should look like it's true. If you have been united with Jesus, this unity should be exemplified in your lives. But as he mentions in Philippians 1:17 and as he implies in 1:27, the wrench in the gears of Christian unity is individual self-interest and pride. And that's where he goes next: "Do nothing from selfish ambition or conceit" (Phil. 2:3).

Do nothing from. No matter what you do, no matter where you go, no matter what you're a part of, what he says after those three words cannot be a motivating factor for Christians. Ever.

The first forbidden motivation is "selfish ambition." Nothing must be done from a place of selfish ambition. So woe to us if we're thinking, *Well, they're making this amount of money, so I've gotta make that amount of money.* Woe to us if we're thinking, *They're at this level of happiness, so I've gotta be a little bit happier than them. If they live in a big house, I've gotta have a bigger house.* It's not just keeping up with the Joneses, as sinful as that is—it's living in such a way as to say,

"In your face, Joneses!" Some translations render *selfish ambition* as "rivalry." It is living as if Christ hasn't settled the score. As if we have not already been given the victory in Christ. As if we haven't already received the infinite riches of the eternal Christ. That sort of thing? Have nothing to do with it. Do nothing from it.

Next is something similar but slightly different: do nothing from conceit. So if selfish ambition is thinking, *I've got to beat them,* conceit is like being a sore loser when you don't. Conceit is about appearances, about saving face. Conceit is like pretentiousness, a pride that connects our feelings to our image. So do you compare yourself to others and become bitter when you think you don't measure up? Do you struggle with envy, jealousy, anger, or malice because you keep seeing the successes or joys of others and compare them with your own (perceived or actual) failures? Do you find yourself despising other people?

Have you ever felt happy when somebody "gets theirs"? There's a big scary German word for that: *schadenfreude.* It basically means taking pleasure when something bad happens to somebody else. This feeling is at the heart of your laughter when you watch guys get hit in the crotch on *America's Funniest Home Videos.* But it's the work of a black heart of hatred in real life, when we take perverse joy in seeing our neighbor fall flat on his or her face. We justify and mask our hatred by reasoning that such failures are what the other people deserve or are good for their humility. But *schadenfreude* is bad for ours. Conceit. It's being conceited. It's putting on airs because we've put ourselves on the throne. We become the arbiter of who's worthy and who's not.

Do nothing, then, from either selfish ambition or conceit. Disobeying this command is self-idolatry. Instead, "in humility count others more significant than yourselves" (Phil. 2:3).

If you don't think that's hard, I don't think you're human. Or else, you have never done any honest introspection and looked at your own heart. And to make sure you don't misunderstand him, Paul doubles down in verse four: "Let each of you look not only to his own interests, but also to the interests of others."

Now, these two behaviors—considering others more significant than yourself, and not looking only to your own interests—will not be produced by a prideful heart or from a daily walk rooted in arrogance. In the end, selfish ambition and conceit come from the idolatrous belief that we are due more than we have received and that we're worthy of more honor than we're getting.

This selfish conviction is the real sin beneath every other sin. It was the *original* original sin. When the serpent tempted Adam and Eve, he did it ultimately with self-exaltation: "You will be like God," he said. And every moment we operate out of selfish ambition and conceit, every time we think of ourselves as better than others or look only to our interests, we are essentially saying, "I am God."

As I said, the dynamic of God's glory and man's lowliness is so prevalent in the Bible that if you wring it out, these themes would be the bulk of what you would see. We see one example in Mary's Magnificat in Luke 1. An angel shows up and tells Elizabeth that she's going to have a baby. Elizabeth is old—too old, she figures, to be having a baby. But she finds out that she's pregnant. Then the angel appears a couple of months later to Mary and tells Mary that she is going to give birth to Jesus, the Son of God. Mary is thinking, *How is that possible? I'm a virgin.* The angel tells her that the Holy Spirit conceived the child in her womb. So she goes to visit Elizabeth. And it's in the exchange between these two astounded ladies that we get some of the most profound pieces of literature in our sacred text.

> In those days Mary arose and went with haste into the hill country, to a town in Judah, and she entered the house of Zechariah and greeted Elizabeth. And when Elizabeth heard the greeting of Mary, the baby leaped in her womb. And Elizabeth was filled with the Holy Spirit, and she exclaimed with a loud cry, "Blessed are you among women, and blessed is the fruit of your womb! And why is this granted to me that the mother of my Lord should come to me?" (Luke 1:39–43)

First, did you notice how Elizabeth calls the unborn child in Mary's womb "Lord"? She's worshipping the baby in Mary's womb! What an incredible faith, and what a powerful biblical support for both the Incarnation and the personhood of the unborn. But let's continue reading as Elizabeth continues exulting:

> For behold, when the sound of your greeting came to my ears, the baby in my womb leaped

for joy. And blessed is she who believed that there
would be a fulfillment of what was spoken to her
from the Lord. (Luke 1:44–45)

What is happening in Mary's womb is so integral to the fulfillment of prophecy, to the future of mankind—*indeed, to the future
of the cosmos*—that it caused John the Baptist to worship in utero!
Before we get into Mary's response to this, in order to make better
sense of it, let's ponder for a moment the height and depth of this
extraordinary moment.

Over the last ten years I've had the opportunity to travel overseas
quite a bit. Something really weird that happens to me every time, as
I leave my wife and children and go to the other side of the world, is
when I pick up the phone and I want to talk to Lauren, but then I
realize that while it's three in the afternoon where I am, it's four in the
morning where she is. While I'm in my home in Dallas, I am rarely
aware of how big, how vast the world is. I'm just not. It doesn't enter
my mind. While I'm sleeping, there's a whole side of the planet where
it's daytime. I just don't think about how big and massive the world
is. But if I go to Asia and experience something cool, I want to pick
up the phone and call my wife to tell her—and then I realize I can't
because it's four in the morning. You know, everybody's relationship
with their spouse is a little different. My wife simply doesn't care until
the sun comes up. It wouldn't matter if I raise a guy from the dead.
If I wake her up on the phone to tell her, she'll be like, "You coulda
told me that in the morning." So I have to wait to call her. And in that
moment I'm aware of just how massive planet Earth is.

If I roll that out—*if I roll that thought all the way out*—and go beyond just the fact that right now, in this very moment, there are millions of people who are laughing, crying, at the heights of emotional joy and at the depths of emotional pain; and going further, there are people right now breathing their last breath, while at the same time someone's giving birth to their first child, while at the same time somebody's eating dinner, while at the same time someone's eating breakfast … it boggles the mind. The world is big. And if you roll *that* realization out to our consideration of the universe, realizing that right now there's a planet hundreds of millions of light-years from here that exists under the sovereign control and might and power of God? Well, then, you start to understand a little bit of what David says to God:

> When I look at your heavens, the work of your
> fingers,
> the moon and the stars, which you have set
> in place,
> what is man that you are mindful of him,
> and the son of man that you care for him?
> (Ps. 8:3–4)

This wonderful awe, this mental discombobulation is what comes out of Mary in her encounter with Elizabeth. God is shaping the apex of human history through the fruit of Mary's womb: creation, fall, redemption, consummation. All of it turns on the Son of God, the infant gestating in Mary's uterus. How does God decide to become incarnate and usher in the kingdom, overthrow the Devil, kill sin, and restore all things? By entering an obscure part of the world, disrupting the lives of an elderly lady and a teenage virgin, neither of whom should be pregnant. And out of this staggering juxtaposition of God's glory and human lowliness erupts this prayerful poetry:

> My soul magnifies the Lord,
>> and my spirit rejoices in God my Savior,
> for he has looked on the humble estate of his
>> servant.
>> For behold, from now on all generations
>>> will call me blessed;
> for he who is mighty has done great things for
>> me,
>> and holy is his name.
> And his mercy is for those who fear him
>> from generation to generation.
> He has shown strength with his arm;
>> he has scattered the proud in the thoughts
>>> of their hearts;
> he has brought down the mighty from their
>> thrones
>> and exalted those of humble estate;
> he has filled the hungry with good things,
>> and the rich he has sent away empty.
> He has helped his servant Israel,

> in remembrance of his mercy,
> as he spoke to our fathers,
> to Abraham and to his offspring forever.
> (Luke 1:46–55)

This praise song is no mere intellectual exercise. It rises up from the depths of Mary's soul. She tells us that in the very first line. So there is deep wisdom in the song. It reveals how God handles those who fear Him. Firstly, they see their place in the light of His glory. Godly fear is profoundly and deeply humbling. But Mary tells us something else as well, something we see Paul going on to address in Philippians 2.

GODLY FEAR RECEIVES MERCY

Mary sings, "His mercy is for those who fear him from generation to generation" (Luke 1:50). How does God handle the humble fearers of Him? *With mercy.*

The Scriptures say here that God has mercy on those who stand in awe, who step a little more gingerly in His presence, who might be a little nervous. It's not just Mary who confirms this. Zacchaeus was a wee little man, right? And a wee little man was he. He climbed up in a sycamore tree, for the Lord he wanted to see. (That's catchy; we should sing it.)

Zacchaeus is a tax collector, which means he is raising money for an occupying Roman force that has raped, murdered, and slaughtered men, women, and children by the thousands. So that's why many Jews are furious when Jesus hangs out with the tax collectors. And this miserable excuse for a human being, Zacchaeus, is trying to get a glimpse of Jesus, but he's trying to be inconspicuous, which is exactly what you aren't when you climb a tree to look at somebody. But what does Jesus do? He spots him, calls him out, and invites Himself to Zacchaeus's house, and by the end of dinner Jesus announces, "Salvation has come to this house" (Luke 19:9).

Mercy is given to the tax collector Zacchaeus. Why? Because he feared Jesus. He had respect for the Lion of Judah.

Think of the Canaanite woman who comes up to Jesus, begging Him to deliver her daughter from demonic oppression (Matt. 15:21–28). What Jesus says is very provocative; it even sounds *mean*.

"I'm here for the Jews, not the Gentiles. Why would I throw food to the dogs?"

Yet how did the woman respond? "Yes, Lord, but even the dogs get to eat the scraps off the floor" (vv. 23–27, author's translation).

That is an awe-*full* lowliness. "Yes, Lord, just give me the scraps. That's all I want." What does Jesus do? He heals the woman's daughter on the spot, declaring, "O woman, great is your faith! Be it done for you as you desire" (v. 28). There is mercy for those who fear Him!

One day as Jesus is walking around, a crowd starts to mob Him. A woman with a bleeding disorder just reaches out and grabs the fringe of His robe. She does not count herself worthy to speak to Jesus, and she's somewhat afraid of what might happen if she directly approaches Him. Jesus feels power leave His body, so He stops and asks, "Who touched me?" The woman emerges, trembling: "I did" (Mark 5:30, author's translation). Jesus says, "Daughter, your faith has made you well; go in peace, and be healed of your disease" (v. 34). There is mercy for those who fear Him.

Perhaps the most vivid example is the repentant thief hanging on his own cross next to Jesus. The Lord is being mocked and spit upon, jeered even by one of the condemned men hanging next to Him. But the other crucified thief, the one who has had a startling change of heart during his torture and proximity to Jesus, rebukes his compatriot: "Do you not fear God, since you are under the same sentence of condemnation? And we indeed justly, for we are receiving the due reward of our deeds; but this man has done nothing wrong" (Luke 23:40–41). The man asks Jesus to remember him when the kingdom comes.

Jesus replies, "Today you will be with me in Paradise" (v. 43).

The thief has had no chance to atone for his sins, no chance to do enough good works to outweigh his bad works. Indeed, even if he had a million lifetimes to do so, it wouldn't be enough. What does he have to offer Jesus? Fear, awe, respect, worship. And God's grace saves him. God has mercy for those who fear Him.

As Paul develops his thoughts on the worthy life in the opening verses of Philippians 2, it is clear that God gives unfathomable blessings to the humble and lowly (vv. 8–11), beginning with His Son, who had no sin to repent of and yet nevertheless submitted to the will of the Father in reverence and self-emptying. Those who fear Christ receive the mercy of salvation precisely because the perfect submission of Christ to the Father is credited to them.

GODLY FEAR RECEIVES EXALTATION

The godly fear that humbles us and receives mercy does not keep us in a nervous or timid state. There is real power in this fear, real grounds for eternal confidence. As we continue reflecting on Mary's Magnificat, notice how she transitions from mercy to strength:

> He has shown strength with his arm;
>> he has scattered the proud in the thoughts
>>> of their hearts;
> he has brought down the mighty from their
>> thrones
>> and exalted those of humble estate. (Luke
>> 1:51–52)

We will look at God's scattering the proud in our next chapter, but for now let's exult in the humbling, merciful exaltation there is to be had in the gospel of Jesus Christ. "He has … exalted those of humble estate": it's another recurring truth of Scripture. Consider the following verses:

> Whoever exalts himself will be humbled, and whoever humbles himself will be exalted. (Matt. 23:12)

Everyone who exalts himself will be humbled, but the one who humbles himself will be exalted. (Luke 18:14)

Humble yourselves before the Lord, and he will exalt you. (James 4:10)

Humble yourselves, therefore, under the mighty hand of God so that at the proper time he may exalt you. (1 Peter 5:6)

It's a rare occurrence in the Bible, actually, to see God exalting a strong, capable, and brilliant person in any significantly enduring way. God instead chooses to use nobodies. The way He appears to operate is like this: "Let Me find the most obscure moron I can and fill that person with My power." When Nathan is sent to Jesse to anoint one of his sons as king, Jesse puts all of his sons in front of the prophet. All but one. He doesn't even think to get his son David. Why? Because David's playing his harp somewhere, and when you think "warrior king," you don't think "guy in a field, playing a harp." But eventually they retrieve David, and Nathan anoints him king.

Do you remember who was king at the time? Saul. Do you know what the Bible says about Saul? He's a foot taller than anyone else in Israel. He's the best hunter and the best warrior in the nation. But God wants the guy in the field who's playing the harp. He exalts those of lowly estate.

Consider Moses as well. Moses has some things going for him, but he is also a stutterer and a murderer. Yet God anoints him and empowers him to be the leader of the children of Israel.

Probably my favorite example by far is that of Peter. I love watching Peter throughout the New Testament. The fact that Peter exists always infuses my life with hope, because Peter is a guy who can never quite figure it out, not even after the Holy Spirit fills him. Even after the church takes off and starts growing, Paul rebukes him because of his hypocrisy about Gentiles when the Jews come to dinner.

I believe that if Jesus had tried to assemble a dream team of the best and brightest, He never would have picked Peter for His missionary team. This disciple tends to be hotheaded, he speaks before he thinks, and he seems generally slow on the uptake, both intellectually and spiritually. But Peter is the dummy on whom Jesus says He's going to build His church (Matt. 16:18).

This guy who is constantly failing Christ, who constantly blunders, is ultimately exalted, used as an apostle and a missionary to the Jews. He goes to heaven after being crucified himself, and someday he will receive a glorified body. Despite his sins, his faithful, godly fear has been credited to him as righteousness.

What does the exaltation of the humble look like? The Magnificat fills in some details:

> He has filled the hungry with good things,
>   and the rich he has sent away empty.
> He has helped his servant Israel,

> in remembrance of his mercy,
> as he spoke to our fathers,
> to Abraham and to his offspring forever.
> (Luke 1:53–55)

The empowering exaltation received by the godly and fearful essentially consists of three things: *resources, rescue,* and *relationship.*

I love the promise that God will fill the hungry with good things. Not just with food, of course, but with abundant blessings and resources. When we are saved, we receive the greatest treasure that exists—Christ Himself—which is worth losing all things for. But the spiritual math is funny: "He who did not spare his own Son but gave him up for us all, how will he not also with him graciously give us all things?" (Rom. 8:32). Or consider Matthew 6:33: "But seek first the kingdom of God and his righteousness, and all these things will be added to you." All who come to Christ with reverent humility and godly fear will receive infinite satisfaction, blessings upon blessings. In His fullness, John says, we get grace upon grace (John 1:16).

We receive not just the resources of the infinite gifts of grace in Christ, however, but also eternal rescue. "He has helped his servant Israel," Mary sings (Luke 1:54). Yes! He helped us firstly and most importantly by forgiving our sins and rescuing us from sin and death. But He helps us in giving us His Spirit, our Comforter and Counselor, who works through us and leads us into the truth. The Spirit is our guarantee of exaltation (2 Cor. 1:22; 5:5).

And more than resources and rescue—we also receive relationship. When we approach God through Christ in humility and spiritual poverty, owning up to our lowly estate and committed to repentance and childlike trust, the Father does not consign us to an eternity of walking on eggshells. In her song, Mary claims that the God who spoke to our covenant father Abraham and the patriarchs will speak to the covenant children forever. The Father reconciles us to Himself, adopts us in love, and shares the honor of His Son with us, making us the siblings of Jesus. Because of this, we may, like the proverbial (and biblical) lamb, lay down with the lion. The author of Hebrews puts it this way: "Let us then with confidence draw near to the throne of grace, that we may receive mercy and find grace to help in time of need" (4:16).

God may be looking for sniveling wimps of all kinds, but sniveling wimpery is not His vision for the eternal family. His plan for us is beyond what we dare imagine.

Who does God exalt? He exalts those who fear His name. God exalts those who approach Him with reverence, self-emptiness, and ownership of their spiritual bankruptcy. And when godly fear humbles us, God in His mercy will exalt us.

In fact, Paul says that if we will receive the humility of Christ, we will shine in the world here today and be filled with the godly kind of pride in the world to come (Phil. 2:1–16).

As we consider the type of person God exalts, however, we must not get ahead of our fleshly selves. There is some dying to be done, and for that, we must pay very close attention to how God handles the proud.

CHAPTER FOUR

WHAT THE
HUMBLE SEEK

For they all seek their own interests, not
those of Jesus Christ. (Phil. 2:21)

At The Village Church where I am a pastor, I wear blue jeans and rarely tuck in my shirt, and that kind of outfit seems to be standard issue for most in our church community. We're not trying to make any kind of statement in dressing like that. It's just what we do; it's what we are. We're casual when it comes to our clothes. But one year, I decided to class myself up a bit for our Christmas Eve service. I went to my closet and found some slacks from a couple of years ago that I could still fit into, and I put on a nice dress shirt. It was red—Christmas-y red. And I tucked it in. Can't say I enjoyed it all that much, but I did it. Just thought I'd dress a little special for this special service. Then I went to church and preached our Christmas Eve services.

The day after Christmas I got an email from a young woman in our congregation—a pretty scathing email essentially calling me a sellout. Her message amounted to this:

> I grew up in a church where you had to wear dress clothes every Sunday. You had to wear a suit if you were a man. You had to wear a dress if you were a woman. And all the focus was on our external appearances, and we felt judged if we didn't measure up. It was very superficial and legalistic. And this is one of the things I've loved about attending The Village: how we're free-form and casual and don't try to outdo one another in dressing up. But, Matt, on Christmas Eve you sold out.

I sold out, she said, because I wore nice pants and tucked in my red dress shirt. Can we be honest about what happened here? All this woman did was change the dress code. That's all. She went from rejecting the idea that if you loved the Lord you'd wear suits to accepting the idea that if you loved the Lord you wouldn't. She really just said the same thing the church of her youth told her when she was young, just about a different style of dress.

The reality beneath her irritation was that her hyper-religious and legalistic parents had wounded her heart, and instead of doing business with that wound, she started lashing out at what she perceived to be the enemy. And that is just one example on top of more serious examples. What do we make of it when in a marriage situation one partner says, "This isn't working. I think we need to get help. I think we need to get counseling. I think we need to go see somebody at the church," and their spouse responds with, "No, we're all right. We'll be all right. I'll do better. We'll work it out"?

In both cases, there is a mental and emotional reality at work beneath the words and postures. It is, fundamentally, pride. Pride says, "I have it figured out. I've got this." It's an assertion of independence and self-allegiance and special knowledge, the kind you think you get from forbidden fruit. This phenomenon is what Mary refers to in the Magnificat when she says that God "has scattered the proud in the thoughts of their hearts" (Luke 1:51).

Being locked up in the prison of our own prideful hearts—what a scary thought. This word *thoughts* in the Greek has more the sense of *imagination*. God scattered the proud in the *imagination* of their hearts. Mary's words foreshadow what Paul writes in Romans 1:21–24:

> For although they knew God, they did not honor him as God or give thanks to him, but they became futile in their thinking, and their foolish hearts were darkened. Claiming to be wise, they became fools, and exchanged the glory of the immortal God for images resembling mortal man and birds and animals and creeping things.
>
> Therefore God gave them up in the lusts of their hearts to impurity.

You will find, if you seriously study Scripture, that outside of the idea of hell, there is no more terrifying idea in the Bible than God setting you free to run in the imagination of your heart.

One of the dangerous problems with being stuck in the imagination of our hearts is that we'll never really be able to deal with the sin in our lives because we're always finding its source in other people instead of looking deep into ourselves for the true issue. So what ends up happening is that we start blaming others, justifying ourselves, and living this really weird life where we've got this long, boring story about how everybody's done us wrong. We turn ourselves into martyrs. And all along, we're never able to recognize our own culpability in our sin or our own responsibility to love, forgive, and strive to be at peace with all people as much as possible. Look, maybe you are the first human being legitimately betrayed by everyone you've ever known. It happens. But it could be that there are some deep heart issues that you need to submit to the Lord. Keep a close watch on your heart, because it is so easy for the proud to get lost in the imagination of their hearts.

May I give you one clue to whether this might be you? Did you just read all that and immediately begin thinking of others who should read it to get straightened out? I don't want to be too bold here—*oh, who am I kidding? Sure, I do*—but I would just say that if you're thinking right now, *Oh, I know who's stuck in the imagination of their heart*, then yeah, I think I might know too.

You.

The proud aren't truly seeking the way of Christ because their vision is filled with the self-centered movie playing on the IMAX screen of their darkened hearts.

CHASING WIND

Sometimes in the evangelical church I get nervous because of the way the Bible talks about rich people. Not because I'm rich but because I'm kind of fond of rich people coming to my church. But the Bible just lays it on really thick: "Hey, rich guy—it's gonna be really difficult, man."

Probably the most famous lines are these:

> Truly, I say to you, only with difficulty will a rich person enter the kingdom of heaven. Again I tell you, it is easier for a camel to go through the eye of a needle than for a rich person to enter the kingdom of God. (Matt. 19:23–24)

The Bible says a lot about the dangers of riches, so if you preach the Bible, you end up preaching the dangers of riches quite a bit— and I always feel like people who have done well for themselves always leave church with their tails tucked between their legs. You know, maybe they're getting into their Benz or whatever and just feel ashamed, thinking, *I'm sorry I own nice things*. But while the Bible warns us about riches, it doesn't do so because money is itself inherently bad. It's not sinful to be wealthy, in other words. I think the Bible is going after our hearts. And the temptations for people who have money are peculiar, strong temptations. Once you've received a lot of money—whether you earned it, inherited it, or won it—it becomes very easy to believe you *deserve* that money. And once you're in entitlement mode, it takes no effort at all to believe you're entitled to *more* than you currently have. It doesn't have to be money in the mix either; it could be power or respect or anything else to which we feel entitled. And the reason the rich go away empty is because everything they're trying to find fulfillment in, *they weren't meant to find fulfillment in.*

In Ecclesiastes we find the concept of chasing the wind (or "striving after wind"—1:14). Solomon writes things like, "I threw parties that were so big that we had to kill, you know, a thousand cows just to feed everybody. I threw parties so big that we needed thousands of barrels of wine. And you know what? Vanity. Meaningless. I planted forests and gardens, built houses and temples—you couldn't get more successful than me in business. You know how it ended? Vanity. It's meaningless. I got massages every day. I got the best cook. I had a lot of wives and a lot of concubines. I had more success in every area of life than you will ever have. You know how it ends? Vanity, vanity, it's all vanity."

And the reason the rich so often go away empty is because many of them constantly want more of that which will never fill them. As they're set free to run in the imagination of their prideful hearts, their only option is to keep running. *And running.* And running and running. Because it's like chasing the wind.

The prophet Isaiah says, "Why do you spend your money for that which is not bread, and your labor for that which does not satisfy?" (Isaiah 55:2). We often say things like this:

- If I just get this job, my life will be perfect.
- If I can just get a boyfriend or a girlfriend or a husband or a wife, he or she will complete me.
- If I just make more money, life will be so much easier.
- If I just get this phone, my life will be better.

When we do get what we desire, we find that the goalpost moved. We envision arriving at a particular place of contentment only to find that it's constantly out of our reach. It's a mirage, like an oasis in the desert. We're chasing the wind.

Worse than being released to run on the treadmill of our striving in the prison of our prideful hearts is this: God is opposed to the proud. If you are chasing the wind, God is adamantly *against* you.

We see this all throughout Scripture:

- Proverbs 6:16–17 says that God hates haughty eyes.
- In Proverbs 8:13, God says, "Pride and arrogance ... I hate."
- Proverbs 16:5 says, "Everyone who is arrogant in heart is an abomination to the LORD; be assured, he will not go unpunished."

• James 4:6 says that God opposes the proud.

Are you getting the picture? If you do things out of what Paul calls selfish ambition and conceit, God says, "You are my enemy."

"But," God says to the humble in heart, "I'm with you. And I am *for* you."

Hearing God's word on this issue is important, and I think it is the necessary examination of every heart, every day. Do you trust Him? Do you honor Him? Do you really fear Him? More deeply than that, can you walk in blessing and humility in the midst of great difficulties or suffering?

Can you get sick and yet praise His name? Can you lose all your money and yet praise His name? Can you lose a loved one and yet praise His name?

This is the question: Are you using God to get something from Him? Or is God Himself the goal of your striving?

SEEKING THE CROSS

Returning to Philippians 2:3–4, let's consider Paul's instructions again:

> Do nothing from selfish ambition or conceit, but in humility count others more significant than yourselves. Let each of you look not only to his own interests, but also to the interests of others.

Interestingly enough, the word *interests* isn't actually there in the Greek text. It's a filler word. There is an openness implied in that line: "Let each of you look not only to his own _____." Fill in the blank. So basically, how this really reads is, "Let each of you look not only to his own house, job, money, family, and friends, but also to the house, job, money, family, and friends of others."

But where does that all-encompassing interest in the needs of others come from? What is the foundation or the motivation of a life that's not built on selfish ambition and conceit but instead on service to and sacrifice for others? Paul tells us:

> Have this mind among yourselves, which is yours in Christ Jesus, who, though he was in the form of God, did not count equality with God a thing to be grasped, but emptied himself, by taking the form of a servant, being born in the likeness of men. And being found in human form, he humbled himself by becoming obedient to the point of death, even death on a cross. Therefore God has highly exalted him and bestowed on him the name that is above every name, so that at the name of Jesus every knee should bow, in heaven and on earth and under the earth, and every tongue confess that Jesus Christ is Lord, to the glory of God the Father. (Phil. 2:5–11)

The foundation, the motivation of a life of humility, is the example of Jesus Christ's humble life and sacrificial death on the cross.

The Bible tells us that Jesus, who was very involved in the act of creation, is also involved in the act of sustaining creation. Colossians 1:17 says, "He is before all things, and in him all things hold together." And Hebrews 1:3 says, "He upholds the universe by the word of his power." So follow where I'm going here. When the Romans arrest Jesus, they grab Him with hands that He not only created but was, at the time, sustaining. In essence, the power they use to grab Him comes from Him. With muscles that He powers, they stretch their hands back and slap His face. They use the glands that He controls to work up the saliva to spit on Him. They nail Him with metal that He created to a tree that He spoke into existence. And He is able to stop it at any moment.

Do you remember when Peter pulls his sword and whacks off the ear of one of the men arresting Jesus? Jesus picks the ear up, throws it back on the guy's head, fully healed, and the guy *still* arrests Jesus. What does Jesus say? "Peter, put away the sword. He who lives by the sword dies by the sword" (Matt. 26:52, author's translation). And then: "Don't you know at any moment I could call out to My father and have at My disposal twelve legions of angels? No one's taking My life from Me. I'm laying it down" (v. 53, author's translation).

So what is a life of humility based on? A life of humility is based on the cross of Jesus Christ, which tells us that Jesus could have chosen to do *none* of it but decided to endure *all* of it.

Now, look at what happens when we live that way—when we're lowly, when we're humble, when we're considering others better than ourselves:

> Therefore, my beloved, as you have always obeyed, so now, not only as in my presence but much more in my absence, work out your own salvation with fear and trembling, for it is God who works in you, both to will and to work for his good pleasure. (Phil. 2:12–13)

Paul acknowledges here that this isn't natural. What would be natural is to look out for yourself. Selfish ambition and conceit. That would be natural.

Paul talks about an all-out denial of self, a death of self. That is why he turns to the cross. And because none of us turn to the cross naturally, Paul reminds us of the gospel of grace. God in His power grants us in His great love the supernatural ability to seek the cross.

He does this by first giving us the mind of Christ. In Philippians 2:5, when the apostle says, "Have this mind among yourselves," he's not just saying, "Try hard to think like Jesus." He tells us that we have this mind. It is part of the gift of the gospel. It is an act of grace. He says that the mind of Christ "is yours in Christ Jesus" (v. 5). You have this mind, in other words. So use it.

Second, Paul tells the church to work out its salvation with fear and trembling (2:12), but he won't disconnect that difficult command from its gracious empowering: "For it is God who works in you" (2:13). The sin you do? Natural. The good you do for others? Supernatural. Always remember the gospel, so you won't forget that God will not expect something of you that He won't both empower you to obey and forgive you for not obeying.

Always, always, always seek the cross. It is there that we see our example for service and sacrifice to others. It is there that we get the power to serve and sacrifice for others. And it is there that we receive forgiveness when we fail in serving and sacrificing for others.

PURSUING CHRIST

You and I as Christians are not meant to cease chasing the wind and commence seeking the cross so that we can make much of ourselves. That is still selfish ambition and conceit. There are some in the church who are very good at presenting the appearance of humility and sacrifice, all for selfish, vainglorious reasons. They enjoy their reputations as servants more than they enjoy the gospel. So we must remember the prayer of John the Baptist: "He must increase, but I must decrease" (John 3:30). The pursuit of the cross is ultimately a pursuit of Christ.

Paul continues his admonition along these lines:

> Do all things without grumbling or disputing, that you may be blameless and innocent, children of God without blemish in the midst of a crooked and twisted generation, among whom

you shine as lights in the world, holding fast
to the word of life, so that in the day of Christ
I may be proud that I did not run in vain or
labor in vain. Even if I am to be poured out as
a drink offering upon the sacrificial offering of
your faith, I am glad and rejoice with you all.
Likewise you also should be glad and rejoice
with me. (Phil. 2:14–18)

Is he not considering them better than himself? Of course he
is. He is willing to be poured out as a sacrifice if it will increase the
faith of the Philippian church. He is in fact "glad" to sacrifice in
this way. Why? So that they will think Paul is great? No, though of
course they will. *So that they will know Christ is great.*

Paul gives us two more examples of seeking Christ through
humility and sacrifice. The first is here:

I hope in the Lord Jesus to send Timothy to you
soon, so that I too may be cheered by news of you.
For I have no one like him, who will be genuinely
concerned for your welfare. For they all seek their
own interests, not those of Jesus Christ. But you
know Timothy's proven worth, how as a son with
a father he has served with me in the gospel. I hope
therefore to send him just as soon as I see how it
will go with me, and I trust in the Lord that shortly
I myself will come also. (Phil. 2:19–24)

Timothy is one of Paul's examples of genuine concern for the Philippians' spiritual well-being and growth. For his part, Timothy is willing to leave his father in the faith to go to Philippi so he can bring back good news to cheer Paul's heart. There are two things at work here: Timothy's deep and abiding love for Paul because of the cross of Christ, and Timothy's deep and genuine concern for the church in Philippi because of the cross of Christ.

Timothy is a selfless man. And here is another example:

> I have thought it necessary to send to you Epaphroditus my brother and fellow worker and fellow soldier, and your messenger and minister to my need, for he has been longing for you all and has been distressed because you heard that he was ill. Indeed he was ill, near to death. But God had mercy on him, and not only on him but on me also, lest I should have sorrow upon sorrow. I am the more eager to send him, therefore, that you may rejoice at seeing him again, and that I may be less anxious. So receive him in the Lord with all joy, and honor such men, for he nearly died for the work of Christ, risking his life to complete what was lacking in your service to me. (Phil. 2:25–30)

Epaphroditus reckons that his life is secondary to Paul being encouraged and the church at Philippi growing into a mature faith.

Why? "For the work of Christ." He, like Timothy, has the mind of Christ, which is theirs through union with Christ. They risk their lives, knowing that Paul has risked his, because they know that ultimately they are totally secure in Jesus. If this service and sacrifice will make Jesus look big, if it will fulfill Jesus's purposes, if it will communicate Jesus to the church and to the world, they are all for it.

Now, let's try to make this practical. Here's a good litmus test: In your world, do people have souls? I know that sounds like a simple question. Let me put it into context. When you sit down at a restaurant, as a believer in Christ, and a young woman or young man waits on you, do you think of him or her as having a soul? As being a spiritual creature? Or are you thinking, *Just give me my drink and take my order and hurry up*? Or do you recognize the image of God in that person? Are you able to encourage, love, and serve your servers, even in a situation as simple as that?

What about in the community of faith?

When I first arrived at The Village Church, a weird thing would happen in the parking lot. The lot was built strangely; when it would rain, the far side of the parking lot would flood. Literally, every time after it rained, there would be about four to six inches of standing water. When this happened, Michael Bleecker, who's one of the worship leaders at our church, would park his car right in the middle of this little lake. You can't jump over it. If you park in the middle, the only way to get through it is to walk through the water. Bleecker would get out of his car, carrying his guitar, carrying his bag, and walk through four to six inches of water, getting his shoes soaking wet. You know why he did it? So no one else had to.

The Village Church is in Dallas, Texas. Here's what that means: it means that ten months out of the year it's a 147 degrees. Not really. *But kinda.* We have to watch out for spontaneous combustion in that parking lot. And maybe the most difficult job at The Village is working on the parking team. Each weekend we try to get thousands of people in and out of our parking lots. We are a young church, so the person-to-car ratio isn't in our favor. It is just a big logistical nightmare. So not only is the parking team out in 147-degree weather, but people can get angry with them, and our parking people get told "you're number one" a lot (if you know what I mean). They get ignored. Or sometimes snarled at. It can be a miserable job. But one of our lead pastors serves on the parking team.

We did not implement a rule that says he has to! So why? Why would he do that? He does it to serve Christ and the people of The Village.

Those are just a couple of low-key examples, certainly easy things to do compared to risking one's life in the mission field or risking one's livelihood honoring Christ in the workplace, but they speak to what we seek even when we're trying to be religious.

What about you? Do you approach your community of faith with a heart attitude that says, "How can I serve? How can I sacrifice?"

We must guard our hearts and ask the Spirit to help us lest the church become a consumeristic mess. We can't afford to come in, order our peppermint latte, sit in a massage chair, and have Bible verses wirelessly beamed onto our retinas. Or something like that. It's not what God has for us. Since His heart for us is not about our joy but His glory, it becomes imperative to pay attention to the Scriptures here.

If we don't pay attention, we'll weaken the reality that the church is actually a group of people meant to represent the image of Christ.

To each other and to the world.

Paul's word to the church at Philippi should be a huge antidote to the inclination to walk with a swagger. Instead, we take up our crosses. And in that moment we shine like stars in a crooked and perverse generation. Remember, we're talking about maturity and must pay attention to our hearts as we read. Has this chapter revealed any "developmental delays" in your growth as a follower of Christ? Are there attitudes and actions that need to be laid bare and repented of?

CHAPTER FIVE

THE PASSIONATE
PURSUIT

*But whatever gain I had, I counted as loss
for the sake of Christ. (Phil. 3:7)*

When I think about the background of the three people we connect to in Philippi—Lydia, the slave girl, and the jailer—it seems
to me that each one of them in their own way was indifferent
toward God, perhaps even hostile toward God. And yet God in the
cross through the apostle Paul brought them to Himself, making a
way for them to be justified through no action of their own. What
should be our response to this reality? If there really is a creator
God who all of us have offended, but who despite that offense
covered that offense, removing it for us so that we would have right
standing before Him, wouldn't that be the greatest news in the
history of the universe?

What kind of response to this news would be a proper response?

I think both the Bible and church history help us answer that question.

Ever since my conversion, I have always resonated most with biblical and historical men and women who have demonstrated an angst-filled yearning for more of Jesus. I have never been much drawn in by moralizing, even though I agree that the Bible tells us what to do and what not to do. Instead, I've always been drawn by the grace of God, to a passionate pleading for more of God, to those who echo the groaning of David in Psalm 63:

> O God, you are my God; earnestly I seek you;
>> my soul thirsts for you;
> my flesh faints for you,
>> as in a dry and weary land where there is no
>> water. (v. 1)

This is not David saying, "I want to be a better guy." This is a yearning from his depths. There is in these lines—if you'll understand the sense of the words—a violence, a lust. With an active, soul-deep desperation, David is crying out, "God, I've got to have You." This sense continues:

> So I have looked upon you in the sanctuary,
>> beholding your power and glory.
> Because your steadfast love is better than life,
>> my lips will praise you.

So I will bless you as long as I live;
    in your name I will lift up my hands.
My soul will be satisfied as with fat and rich
    food,
    and my mouth will praise you with joyful
    lips. (vv. 2–5)

For David, God is not some distant grandfather type or some ethereal idea to noodle around with intellectually. God is all-consuming.

When I remember you upon my bed,
    and meditate on you in the watches of the
    night;
for you have been my help,
    and in the shadow of your wings I will sing
    for joy.
My soul clings to you;
    your right hand upholds me. (vv. 6–8)

I love King David because I can resonate with him. In the Psalms he keeps saying things like that. See Psalm 42 for another example. But while you might find on one page of the Psalms David crying out to God, "You're gracious and good and beautiful," literally on the next page he may be saying, "God, where are You? Why have You abandoned me?" In this way he's very much a guy we can relate to.

It's for this reason that John Calvin calls the Psalms an anatomy of the human soul. This book certainly captures our vacillating between highs and lows, the entire human experience of joy and pain, victory and suffering, and, throughout it all, how God is sovereign over and loving to both the exulting soul and the depressed one.

I am fearful that, in general, modern evangelicalism has become uncomfortable with this sense of all-consuming passion for God. We love the feelings in a worship experience, of course, but that's more along the lines of catharsis, sort of a therapeutic approach to worship. David and the other biblical figures who wrote and spoke this way were not pursuing experiences—they were pursuing God. And so when David says in Psalm 42:1–2, "As a deer pants for flowing streams, so pants my soul for you, O God. My soul thirsts for God, for the living God," we turn it into kitsch, cute-ing it up by putting it under a picture of a deer on a T-shirt or coffee mug. But it's not kitschy, and it's not cute. David is in pain. He's crying, "Why can't I get there? Why can't I get more of You?" He does it again in Psalm 27:4: "One thing have I asked of the LORD, that will I seek after: that I may dwell in the house of the LORD all the days of my life, to gaze upon the beauty of the LORD and to inquire in his temple."

Is this desperation something that typifies the church today? Like Moses crying out, "I want to see You, Lord! I want to see Your glory" (Exod. 33:18, author's translation)? Can our singing, our preaching, our prayers, our books, even our blogs and tweets and Facebook updates be said to reflect an all-encompassing yearning for God? This is where Paul is going in Philippians 3. Nothing compares to the Lord. Everything else indeed is rubbish compared to the surpassing worth of having Jesus.

THE GAME YOU ALWAYS LOSE

Paul continues the exultation and exhortation of the previous chapter, which he concluded by holding out Timothy and Epaphroditus as examples of humble sacrifice for the cause of the gospel. Remember that Paul himself is writing this from prison, not sure if he will be released, not sure if he will be executed. He is about to warn the Philippians—but notice what he warns them about. Hint: it's not imperial persecution or suffering.

> Finally, my brothers, rejoice in the Lord. To write the same things to you is no trouble to me and is safe for you. Look out for the dogs, look out for the evildoers, look out for those who mutilate the flesh. For we are the circumcision, who worship by the Spirit of God and glory in Christ Jesus and put no confidence in the flesh. (Phil. 3:1–3)

I am convicted and inspired by the way Paul, writing from such dire circumstances, says, "Eh, it's no trouble." No, look instead at what Paul is warning the Philippians to watch out for: "the dogs."

Who are the dogs? They are the ones who want to mark their faith in Christ by what they do or do not do. And they want to get a list of things that they do well. They want to say, "I'm not as bad as I was in college. I'm not as bad as I was when I first got married. I'm not as bad as *you*." And they want to use that as some sort of evidence of their superior spirituality, their higher-quality goodness, their unassailable morality. They are in fact scattered in the imaginations of their prideful hearts.

Paul says to watch out for that kind of faith. It is empty. Watch out for the kind of teachers and leaders who say, "Just pay attention to me because of the good things I do." And to demonstrate the emptiness of this pursuit, Paul puts his own self up on the scales.

> Though I myself have reason for confidence in the flesh also. If anyone else thinks he has reason for confidence in the flesh, I have more: circumcised on the eighth day, of the people of Israel, of the tribe of Benjamin, a Hebrew of Hebrews; as to the law, a Pharisee; as to zeal, a persecutor of the church; as to righteousness under the law, blameless. (Phil. 3:4–6)

Oh, you think *you* have reason to boast? I have reason to boast all the more. I have never missed Sunday school. I have never missed a Sunday-morning worship service. I read my Bible every day. I've memorized the New Testament. I've shared the gospel with all of my neighbors. I've never said a cuss word besides invented Christian expletives like "Oh, dingbat!" and "Shazbot!" and stuff

THE PASSIONATE PURSUIT

like that. I don't listen to secular music. I've never seen a rated-R movie (that wasn't about Jesus being crucified).

The dogs stay focused on "I do. I don't. I have. I never." And look at what they have done. Look at what they have accomplished.

Paul here, as loudly as he can, is saying, "Who cares? I did all that too. On the scale, I'm even better than *you*!"

"But whatever gain I had, I counted as loss for the sake of Christ" (Phil. 3:7).

Whatever good came from the self-improvement project still didn't earn a lick of grace from God. Because none of it even approached the utter perfection of Jesus. Playing the "I'm good, I'm better" game is like building a moralistic tower of Babel to reach the heavens of the righteousness of Christ. It won't work, and in the end, it leads only to disaster and confusion. It is a losing game.

But let's be honest. Real good can come from never missing Sunday-morning worship. Real good comes from guarding what you watch. Good can come from guarding your life in these ways. But as a means to or measure of our righteousness? These things will always fall short.

Paul is unpacking these reasons for you to violently and lustfully pursue Christ at all costs, because even if you get all of those good, morally superior attainments—if you clean up your life and manage to somehow never struggle ever again—but you never get Jesus, you've totally lost. You've actually attained a whole lot of nothing. In the end, if you look great and sound great and act great, but you don't know Jesus, who cares?

ONLY TO BE FOUND IN HIM

Therefore, Paul says, "Every gain I got I considered as loss for the sake of Christ." In comparison to the infinite gain of Jesus, Paul considers *everything* else negotiable, everything sacrifice-able, everything lose-able.

> Indeed, I count everything as loss because of the surpassing worth of knowing Christ Jesus my Lord. For his sake I have suffered the loss of all things and count them as rubbish, in order that I may gain Christ and be found in him, not having a righteousness of my own that comes from the law, but that which comes through faith in Christ, the righteousness from God that depends on faith—that I may know him and the power of his resurrection, and may share his sufferings, becoming like him in his death, that by any means possible I may attain the resurrection from the dead. (Phil. 3:8–11)

He uses the word *rubbish*, which could be read as garbage, as dung, as excrement. Only this sort of extreme could approach the level of excellence there is to be had in Jesus. The best of our best, without Jesus, looks like a pile of crap compared to Him.

So, Paul's saying, if you are to pursue righteousness, pursue Jesus. Don't let looking good or being better be your goal. Let the goal be Him.

Why should we go hard after Jesus? To know Him.

Since Christ is infinite, there will always be more of Him to be had. Even if you live to be 170, you haven't even begun to unpack the fullness of who He is. There's always more of Him to be had. So Paul's pleading, "Hey, don't get led astray by legalists, and don't get caught up in secondary pursuits."

Know Him!

The men and women who walk with this angst to see and savor Jesus aren't just found in the Bible but throughout Christian history and I hope in the church you currently attend. Let's look at history for a bit.

In Augustine's *Confessions*, he says this:

> But where in all that long time was my free will, and from what deep sunken hiding-place was it suddenly summoned forth in the moment in which I bowed my neck to Your easy yoke and my shoulders to Your light burden, Christ Jesus, my Helper and Redeemer? How lovely I suddenly found it to be free from the loveliness of those vanities, so that now it was a joy to renounce what I had been so afraid to lose. For You cast them out of me, O true and supreme Loveliness, You cast them out of me and took their place in me, You who are sweeter than all pleasure.[1]

Do you hear the echo of biblical angst in those words?

Augustine found God sweeter than any other pleasure, greater than any other joy. His affections involved in his lustful pursuit of sex and other lesser goods were transformed and transferred to his pursuit of God. By God's grace, he began a lustful pursuit of Christ.

We see similar sentiments from other Christian writers:

- "I wish to devote my mouth and heart to you.... [D]o not forsake me, for if I ever should be on my own, I would easily wreck it all."—Martin Luther[2]
- "I thank Thee that this, which is a necessity of my new life, is also its greatest delight. So, I do at this hour feed on Thee."—Charles Spurgeon[3]
- "Herein would I live;—herein would I die;— hereon would I dwell in my thoughts and affections, to the withering and consumption of all the painted beauties of this world, unto the crucifying all things here below, until they become unto me a dead and deformed thing, no way meet for affectionate embraces."—John Owen, on beholding the glory of Christ[4]

The Practice of the Presence of God by Brother Lawrence is probably the most confounding expression that I have read of this pursuit of Christ as better and sweeter. He writes, "I am presently recalled by inward motions so charming and delicious that I am ashamed to mention them."[5] To this day, with all the theological education I have attained, I still have no idea what he's talking about. But I can feel it. There's an angst there. There's a yearning. There is a sense of what Rudolf Otto called the *mysterium tremendum*, the experience of God that is totally other, entirely foreign to us and yet captivating to us, taking us away, transforming us, moving us, stirring us, and spiritually and sweetly discombobulating us.

And not only do men yearn for God in this lustful, violent way, God even says that the natural order is doing this too.

> For the creation waits with eager longing for the revealing of the sons of God. For the creation was subjected to futility, not willingly, but because of him who subjected it, in hope that the creation itself will be set free from its bondage to corruption and obtain the freedom of the glory of the children of God. For we know that the whole creation has been groaning together in the pains of childbirth until now. (Rom. 8:19–22)

Even creation, having been pressed or subjected to futility, is longing to join in with the freedom that's been given to the sons of God, the lifting of decay, the removal of the weight of sin, and the vanquishing of the curse. So now we know why the wolves howl. We know why the whales groan. We know why the trees creak. They, with us, are groaning. There's something intrinsic in creation that remembers what it was like before it was subjected to futility. And so creation itself is eagerly watching the sons and daughters of the King, waiting for the last one to come into the kingdom so that the rocks and trees can be set free.

Why does creation groan? Creation groans for the same reason we do: it longs for the consummation of all things when Christ returns and finally executes eternal justice, restores all things, and establishes His sovereign reign over all the earth. Creation, like us (and because of us), is longing to be found in Christ.

Paul says, "I have suffered the loss of all things and count them as rubbish, in order that I may gain Christ and be found in him" (Phil. 3:8–9). All the persecution, all the suffering, all the pain, all the daily dying to self, and all the wasting away in the flesh is worth it compared to the joy of knowing Jesus, being with Jesus, and becoming like Jesus. The joy of the Lord is Paul's strength, which is why after putting forth the sacrificial examples of his disciples at the end of Philippians 2, Paul begins Philippians 3 by saying, "Finally … rejoice."

If in response to the gospel *now*, we conclude "joy," then at the end of days, whether brought there by death or by the Lord's return, we will experience the concluding joy of eternity as well. *If* we will seek to be found only in Christ.

WHAT MOVES YOU?

We've established that in the Bible, men and women passionately pursued the Lord. We've seen some examples from church history of men describing their passion for knowing Jesus above all things. And we've seen that even creation itself groans for its redemption.

Here is my question: *Why don't we?* Why are we so easily satisfied? Why is this sense of lustful, soul-deep angst so uncommon?

Romans 8 tells us that it's not just creation, but we ourselves who groan in this way. But I don't see a lot of groaning in myself. I find myself far too easily satisfied with my relationship with the Lord, far too easily satisfied with where I am spiritually. Why don't we long for the Lord like David did?

Why are so many of us apparently unconcerned about passages like Matthew 7:21–23?

> Not everyone who says to me, "Lord, Lord," will enter the kingdom of heaven, but the one who does the will of my Father who is in heaven. On that day many will say to me, "Lord, Lord, did we not prophesy in your name, and cast out demons in your name, and do many mighty works in your name?" And then will I declare to them, "I never knew you; depart from me, you workers of lawlessness."

Why aren't we terrified over that text?

Why isn't this a part of who we are?

I think I know why. I didn't have any idea for a while after I was saved, but I think I know why a little bit better now. I think we often misunderstand our faith and put all the weight on our conversion, with very little expectation for what comes afterward. This is what Paul gets at in Philippians 2:12 when he says that we should work out our salvation as God works in us. Do it with fear and trembling, he says. Why? Because he knows that pressing the dominion of the gospel into the deepest reaches of our hearts and lives will involve lots of dying-to-self moments.

It is a fearful, trembling thing to take up the cross. But Jesus says we must do that, so Paul insists we must do it. We can't stop trusting Him at conversion; we must keep trusting Him, walking by faith, feeling the weight of the cross each day, knowing that God is at work in and through us, and believing that our suffering will be worth it. Paul sees the fear and trembling of daily self-denial as a way of "shar[ing] his sufferings, becoming like him in his death" (Phil. 3:10). Paul takes the long view. He knows that if he will daily share in Christ's sufferings, he will, in the end, share in Christ's resurrection (3:11).

Instead, what often happens for us when we come to know the Lord—and usually it comes from a very sincere place—is that our love of God's grace is replaced with a sense of obligation to please Him. It starts with gratitude but easily and naturally turns into trying to pay back a debt—to earn His grace, in other words. We move on to the self-salvation project so rapidly.

Instead we need to ask a question complementary to good works. We need to ask ourselves: *What moves me toward Jesus? What stirs my affections for Jesus Christ?*

What is it that stirs you up to know Him, to love Him, to worship Him? It will probably look different for a lot of people. It will have to involve the Scriptures, because that's how God speaks to us. It will involve prayer, because that's how we speak to God. It involves worship, but we have to remember that worship is bigger and more expansive than singing songs in church. What is it that incorporates the Word and prayer and ultimately builds your heart in worship?

By way of example, let me show you some of the things that stir my affections for Jesus Christ.

One of the first times I became aware of the oddity of how my affections affect my pursuit of Christ was at the funeral of the father of one of my college roommates. The man was a military veteran, so he received a twenty-one-gun salute, the presenting of the colors, and all that. It was a beautiful service.

Afterward, I walked through the graveyard and found the headstone of a guy who died at twenty-five years old. I was about twenty-five myself at the time. I sat down right next to his burial plot and thought about whether his life had looked like mine at the moment he died. Did he have a wife? What were his hopes? Did he picture himself as an old man?

In that moment I became keenly aware of my mortality. I realized very starkly and deeply that I'm going to stand in front of God and give an account for my life, and I cannot in any way clean myself up. I became, in that moment in the graveyard, a better lover of Christ.

I just love early mornings. There's something about how cool it is in the mornings, even in July in Dallas. It's cool. It's quiet. There's something about the smell of good, French-pressed coffee. The smell of coffee at 5:30 a.m. makes me love Jesus more. Sometimes I'll get up early in the morning, press some coffee, and open up my Bible and usually a book by a dead guy (not that there aren't some excellent books being written now). Edwards, Luther, the Reformers, and the Puritans, the way they write, the way they exult in the gospel in their writing, stirs me like nothing else. So for me, an early-morning situation like that is a perfect storm for worship.

Epic movies stir my affections. I love all the great themes and the expansive scenes set to stirring musical scores.

Those are just a few examples of things that stir my affections for Jesus.

If you pay attention to that which stirs your affections for Jesus and His gospel, you will also be able to identify that which robs your affections for Him. For most of us who've been saved for a little while, it's not the so-called "big things" that get us anymore. We don't find a lot of temptation in major stuff. For instance, if I'm on my way out to my car in the parking lot and a guy walks up to me and says, "Hey, you, uh, you want a little black tar heroin?"— that's not something that's going to tempt me very much. I'm not drawing up a list of pros and cons on doing heroin.

No, in fact, the morally neutral temptations are far more apt to rob me of my affections for Jesus Christ, because God's grown me to the place where those "big sins" aren't things that appeal to me anymore. But I can easily justify sinfully indulging in things that are non-sins because they are little things, or what the Song of Solomon might call the "little foxes" that get into the vineyard of my worship of God.

For instance, I can't follow sports too closely. *Isn't that crazy?* I can't follow sports *too closely*, because I will start to care. And, really, how dumb is it to be emotionally affected by how a twenty-one-year-old handles a ball? How dumb is it to have your day ruined because a group of twentysomethings fails you in a game?

I can't watch too much television. I'm not an anti-TV guy, and I'm sure there are some great things on television, but if I watch too much of it, here's what happens to me: I'll unplug from holy things. Before I know it, I'm giggling at things the Lord calls wicked. So I can't watch too much.

Here's another one: even something as simple as sleeping in too long will make me get up in a rush, not center myself on God, not think about Him at all, and begin a day by running through tasks.

Those are some things that rob my affections. What moves you? And what dampens your fervor for Christ?

If we're living life in a pursuit of Jesus Christ, as opposed to a gospel-denying pursuit of self-improvement, we will answer those questions in ways that push us further into the gospel, not further into legalism. Because the worst thing we can do in figuring out what stirs us and what quenches us is to determine for others that they shouldn't watch TV, or that they must get up early in the morning in order to be godly people. If we do that we are not glorying in Christ but in our behaviors. We've suddenly turned pursuit of Christ into the same badges of honor Paul says we should throw away, consider as rubbish. In other words, we start to worship *worship*.

My friend Bleecker is not like me. He's not going to get up at 5:30 a.m. and read Edwards. And for me to expect him to do that wouldn't be fair. He's going to get up and grab his guitar and sing through the Psalms to the Lord. I'm not going to do that. I think the Lord would be like, "Hey, buddy, put down the guitar and pick up a book. Bless your heart."

This is what we're looking at as we gaze at Christ: getting rid of the baggage, religious or otherwise, that distracts us from Him alone. As Hebrews 12:1 says, "Let us also lay aside every weight, and sin which clings so closely." When we do that, we can run so much faster after Jesus.

He has broken the bonds that held us back. He has set us free. He has given us life. He has given us the empowering Spirit. So run! Make a break for it. Pursue Him and Him alone, with force, oomph, and passion.

Why? To know Him. What stirs your affections for Jesus? What robs you of those affections for Christ? Answering those two questions is serious business, and there is joy to be had once you answer them!

CHAPTER SIX
OWNED

Christ Jesus has made me his own. (Phil. 3:12)

I have two little girls, and I am already terrified for them. I would hate to be a girl in our culture today. Everything seems to revolve around external beauty—and add to that the nonsense the media is constantly communicating to our young girls. If you're paying attention you've probably noticed that every romantic movie, every book, every magazine, and most of a woman's peers make claims like this:

- "I love you because of how I feel when I am with you." (What about when the feelings leave?)
- "I love you because you treat me this way." (What if he treats you poorly once? Does love disappear?)

- "I love you because we never fight." (Then you are not in much of a relationship ... or someone is lying.)

What is love?

I try to express the truth of what love is to my girls every chance I get. One night before bed, I told my daughter Audrey how much I love her, and a thought occurred to me. *Does she actually know why I love her?* I've told her plenty of times that I love her. She nearly always looks back at me and says, "I love you, too." So I asked her: "Do you know why Daddy loves you?"

She was perplexed. I can imagine what was running through her mind. *Because we had fun together? Because I made some good choices today? Because we read books together?* She could not crystallize her thoughts, but I could see her mind racing. Though she wanted desperately to answer my question, she couldn't. I will never forget taking her little face in my hands and watching her look up at me with those adorable eyes that melt me. And I told her, "I love you because you are mine. God gave you to me."

Isn't it nice when someone's love for you is not contingent upon what you do?

Such is the love of God.

GRACE FOR BROKENNESS

God has been very, very gracious to me, because there were some serious issues in my home when I was growing up. Some wicked things happened. And because of my background, I had two pretty serious issues in my mind and heart during those years. One was a temper. The other was lust. These were some pervasive generational things with which I struggled.

But then I came to know Christ. My hope was that He would take those things from me. That's certainly the message I had heard from the pulpit. And when I looked around our church, everybody looked very put together, like they all had it figured out.

Christ powerfully saved me, rescued my heart. I loved Him very much. But it wasn't too long after my conversion experience when I realized that anger and lust were still going to be problems for me. My temper had not left me, and lust was still a viable expression when anger and bitterness crept up in my heart.

The thing that confused me and wounded me for a long time, the thing that even soured me on the church for a while, was this: I felt like I was being taught that in my justification, total sanctification also occurred. I thought that in my salvation, my struggles would go away, and further, that if they weren't removed, it somehow revealed I wasn't actually new in Christ.

But this is simply not true.

Consider what Paul says in Philippians 3:12: "Not that I have already obtained this or am already perfect, but I press on to make it my own, because Christ Jesus has made me his own."

Why is Paul passionately pursuing Jesus? Why should we continue to pursue Him, even after our conversion? Because we are broken people. We are really broken.

It is so helpful here that Paul says, "Not that I've already obtained this." It's comforting, in an odd way, for him to say, "Not that I'm already perfect." Instead, he acknowledges that he still struggles, needs to grow in some areas, and must continue to follow Jesus, and he says this: "I press on."

Think about this verse in relation to your struggles with sin in the Christian life. Whatever your particular sins, the implication here is that there is a right way to struggle and a wrong way to struggle. The wrong way to struggle might be described like this: "Let me control this. Let me manage this." And the right way to struggle might be described like this: *Push headlong into Jesus, and then keep pushing.* Paul says in 2 Corinthians 3:18 that it's by beholding Jesus that we are transformed by degrees into the image of Jesus. Remember the words of the famous hymn: "Turn your eyes upon Jesus / look full in His wonderful face / and the things of earth will grow strangely dim / in the light of His glory and grace."[1]

The broken in Christ must keep pursuing Christ so that Christ's power will break more and more areas of bondage in their lives. Going after this merely through behavior modification simply won't work.

How do you beat sin? We beat sin only by pressing into Jesus, knowing Him, and chasing Him. There is grace upon grace to be had in Him. So much grace, you can't use it all up. If we broken people will come to Christ in faith, we will receive an infinite supply of grace. This is why we pursue Christ above all—because He is more than enough. *He will always be enough.*

And He knows our struggles! He knows we are broken people. He knows we still wrestle with entangling sin. He sympathizes with our weaknesses and temptations. It makes no sense to deny them or cover them up or pretend like they don't exist. We have in Christ the grace that gives us the security to "own" our struggles in front of others. In Christ's grace, there is freedom to be honest and transparent. When we embrace that security and freedom, then we end up pointing others to the only Source of healing and forgiveness. That source is not our self-improvement project, but the finished work of Christ on the cross and out of the tomb.

A GRACE THAT WON'T LET GO

My father was in the military, so my family moved quite a bit when I was growing up. I arrived in Texas via the Bay Area in California. When I was in high school, a guy named Jeff began to share the gospel with me and a few of our friends. Every day, I sat at a table of guys, and Jeff would just use the time to tell us all about his faith. Most of us were familiar with the general arc of the story. We'd heard that there is a creator God who we sinned against. Most of us had heard that He sent His Son to die for us. And we heard that Jesus came back to life so we could go to heaven when we die. But it was just sort of an intellectual or cultural familiarity.

Despite knowing the basics, I had a lot of questions for Jeff. I pressed him with a lot of questions for about a year. I went to church with him, and I have to tell you, church was such a goofy thing to me. In the experience of late 1980s and early 1990s youth ministry, I don't know how anyone came to Christ. It might have been the most uncool period in church history, and I'm totally aware of the Inquisition.

Back then, you'd walk into a youth-group meeting where they're singing, "I got joy down in my heart. Deep, deep down in my heart!" Then someone would call out, "Spell it!" and the entire group would spell *joy* with their bodies.

How in the world did we expect anyone to begin a serious relationship with Jesus in that environment? There was nothing about that experience that made me, as an unsaved high schooler, think, *I want some of this.* But I went anyway, and I listened and heard the gospel.

I had a thousand questions that I needed answered before I'd become a believer, and maybe a couple of them got answered. But I heard the gospel preached. And in an instant—I mean *in an instant*—after that year of asking questions and experiencing that goofy youth group, I suddenly did not care anymore if I had answers to those questions.

Now, I still have questions, some of the same ones I was asking back then, but in the moment I was captivated with Christ's gospel, by the blood of Christ, He opened up my heart and my mind and saved me. The sovereign God of the universe said, "This one is Mine." Over and against all the prerequisites I had invented for placing my faith in God, the Father had placed His Spirit in me.

"I love you because you're Mine," He said.

Let me show you this idea on an epic scale.

Blessed be the God and Father of our Lord Jesus
Christ, who has blessed us in Christ with every
spiritual blessing in the heavenly places, even
as he chose us in him before the foundation of
the world, that we should be holy and blameless
before him. (Eph. 1:3–4)

I've found that the longer someone has been in church, the
more difficult believing this truth becomes. Some people have
been in church for so long, been doing the "be a good Christian"
thing for so long, that the very idea that they were chosen and
determined for blamelessness before they'd started earning credit
is very offensive. In our flesh, we tend to think that our holiness
is the result of our spiritual elbow grease. We intellectually may
agree to the doctrine of *sola gratia*, but we tend to live and act like
we're saved by what Don Whitney calls "sola boot-strappa." That,
however, is not the testimony of Scripture.

Paul continues:

In love he predestined us for adoption as sons
through Jesus Christ, according to the purpose of
his will, to the praise of his glorious grace, with
which he has blessed us in the Beloved. (Eph.
1:4–6)

If you have a tendency to think that there's no way you can
chase Jesus like this, know Jesus like this, walk with Jesus like this,

experience Jesus like this because you've done some awful thing or because you have some shady past or because you still struggle with sin, this text is calling you a liar. It refutes all of that kind of thinking, because it's saying clearly that God rescues the dirty to the praise of His glorious grace. It's the same gracious dynamic in place as when we saw God saying to the little harp-playing shepherd boy David, "You're Mine." To David the murderous adulterer: "You're Mine." To Moses the unqualified, stuttering murderer: "You're Mine." To Paul the murderer: "You're Mine." And in response, Paul becomes the man driven to basically say, "Surely my best efforts are garbage compared to this righteousness given to me totally of grace and promised to me before the beginning of time!" (Phil. 3:8, author's translation).

Why is it that so few "pretty people" without checkered pasts are used mightily in the Scriptures? Because the Bible is primarily about God's grace, not about human cleanliness. What a staggering truth that the holy God of the universe would say, "Mine," about sinners and lay hold of them in love. Paul goes on to say, "In him we have redemption through his blood, the forgiveness of our trespasses, according to the riches of his grace" (Eph. 1:7).

We are redeemed through what? Our efforts? No, Christ's blood. We are forgiven of our sins according to what? Our moral credit? No, the riches of His grace.

And His grace is so rich! Even when I've tried to run from God, it has not gone well for me. It's a weird conundrum, the Christian life—we can either chase Him or be miserable at some level. If we want joy, satisfaction, and peace, we really have no option but Jesus. In John 6, after the crowd leaves Jesus, finding His teaching offensive, He asks His disciples, "Do you want to leave too?" The disciples constantly get things wrong, and they'll struggle with the mission of Jesus for a long time after, but in this moment, they are wise enough to reason this way to the Lord:

"To whom would we go?"

Everywhere else we'd go would be a disaster for us. Any answer but Jesus is no answer at all. And yet, even when we run, His grace reaches us. Of course, sometimes grace looks like getting swallowed by a big fish, but what a joy anyway to know that we cannot outrun God's sovereign love for us. His grace lays hold of us, and His grace will not let us go.

So why don't we yearn? Why don't we long? Why don't we passionately pursue Christ in this way? I think it's because we're trying to manage life according to our own spiritual riches. Paul says in Philippians 3:12, "Not that I have already obtained it," and we're thinking, *Well, we know better than him. He obviously didn't try hard enough. He didn't give 110 percent.*

Paul himself calls such thinking stupid. "Are you so foolish?" he asks in Galatians 3:3. "Having begun by the Spirit, are you now being perfected by the flesh?" No, it is Spirit beginning to end. Which is why in Philippians 2:13, he says that it is God who is working in you the ability to work out your salvation.

Over and over again, we return in our efforts to pursue Christ. There is something right and good about a disciplined life that is built around knowing Jesus more fully, but we must never forget the reality that He has first pursued us. That He has chosen us first (John 15:16). That He loved us first (1 John 4:19). And in doing this, in returning to the total justification we have in Christ, declared from the foundation of the world in the predestining purposes of God, we find the power to press on into our sanctification.

Returning to Philippians 3, we find Paul affirming this dynamic:

> Not that I have already obtained this or am already perfect, but I press on to make it my own, because Christ Jesus has made me his own. Brothers, I do not consider that I have made it my own. But one thing I do: forgetting what lies behind and straining forward to what lies ahead, I press on toward the goal for the prize of the upward call of God in Christ Jesus. Let those of us who are mature think this way, and if in anything you think otherwise, God will reveal that also to you. Only let us hold true to what we have attained. (vv. 12–16)

Paul presses on (present tense) because Christ has made him His own (past tense). The imperative of obedience is grounded in the indicative of the gospel. Paul closes this passage in the same way, after talking about pressing on, forgetting the past, and straining forward—and he answers the upward call, coming back to say, "Only let us hold true to what we have attained." Returning to the gospel over and over again is of vital importance in the pursuit of Christ. We cannot pursue Him passionately otherwise. The gospel is where the power is. It's where the awe is.

We return to the gospel again and again, also, because the fact that God keeps loving us, empowering us, and sanctifying us despite our ongoing troubles and sufferings is in itself very good news.

This brings us to the turning point for everyone in Christian maturity. Will you passionately pursue Christ in the gospel?

I have said for years now that church is the lamest hobby in the universe. Get a boat. Go mountain climbing. Ski. If you're just looking for some kind of self-improvement experience, do something other than church. The church as a self-help center is a terrible thing to devote your life to. I mean, it's on Sunday morning. It's early. You have to stand up a lot. It's a lame, lame, lame hobby.

Is this all you're doing with your Christian life? Finding something to put in the "spiritual" category of your life?

Or can you see the overwhelming truth of God's good news? Do you see that, compared to the infinitely perfect holiness of God, your righteousness is garbage? And do you realize that God loves you eternally to the point that He was willing to put His own holiness into action to forgive, save, and redeem you? In faith, not works, Christ's perfect righteousness is considered yours.

So let us join in with the men and women in Scripture and church history, and with creation itself, in groaning for this gracious God.

Don't stop. Keep pressing on. He has laid hold of you.

And He will not let go.

God help us, for the sake of His name.

CHAPTER SEVEN
NEVER SATISFIED

I press on. (Phil. 3:14)

As I mentioned earlier, I like to read the dead guys. It's one of my favorite things in the world. It just excites me, honestly. I am, for lack of a better word, a studier. It does not bother me to open up the Word of God, grab a pen and paper, open up my computer, and just dig into trying to answer difficult questions and wrestle with difficult texts. Being a studier is one of my strengths.

But in the area of prayer, I am weak. Prayer is laborious for me. In fact, one of my favorite verses is Romans 15:30 in which Paul says, "Strive together with me in your prayers." I think, *Oh, thank God that striving in prayer is biblical.*

Knowing that study is something I do well and that I struggle with heart-level, soul-deep prayer creates in me a holy discontentment about my prayers. I want an intimate relationship with Jesus

Christ. I see in both the Bible and Christian history men and women who pray deep and wide, while my prayers feel shallow and narrow. And so my prayers tend to become, "Lord, I don't want to just study about You. I want to *know* You. I don't want to be a guy who talks about You. I want to be a guy whose heart is after You."

Just being aware of the reality of this weakness in myself helps me lean into the Spirit for strength in the same area. I am promised that when "we do not know what to pray for as we ought, ... the Spirit himself intercedes for us with groanings too deep for words" (Rom. 8:26). I know it's very popular in the business world and even in the church world to say that we ought to only play to our strengths and spend little time on our weaknesses, but I don't see that spirit of efficiency too much in the Bible. We don't get that luxury in our faith. By dwelling in our weaknesses, we can linger with God and rely on His gracious love. And in sorting our strengths from our weaknesses, we can begin to develop the sort of holy discontentment that underlies Paul's instructions to the Philippians to "press on."

Press on, then, in the exercise of introspection. It is important to know yourself really well. It will not help you a bit if you lie when it comes to yourself. In other words, don't lie to yourself about you. Know where you're weak. Know your thoughts. Know the places in your heart that you don't want to give to the Lord. You must build time into your life to become aware of what's really going on in your heart, in your mind, and deep inside of you. Constantly ask yourself good diagnostic questions about areas of doubt and disbelief.

We're getting even more practical now. A holy discontentment is good because it keeps driving us into Christ for rest in Him and the blessing of Him. As we've seen, we want to identify the things that stir our affections for Christ, and we also want to thereby identify the things that quench them. Now let's examine some ways we can stay in the crosshairs of this holy discontentment, that we might be never satisfied with ourselves and can keep finding our satisfaction in Him.

FINDING GOOD EXAMPLES

An intimate familiarity with our weaknesses would do wonders for our sense of holy discontentment. Another primary way to stay dissatisfied with ourselves is to continually measure ourselves against the holiness of Christ, because we will always fall short. As long as we maintain our grasp of the gospel and keep attuned to the grace of God, these sorts of exercises can be healthy, because they keep us both humble and confident: *humble in ourselves and confident in Christ.* If we simply compare ourselves to Jesus but never make the step of believing that His goodness is imputed to us by faith, we will remain mired in defeat and shame.

So if we're always tuned to the grace of God, we can fearlessly examine our weaknesses and, in a healthy way, regularly contrast our imperfection with the perfection of Jesus.

And there's still another way to avoid the spiritual plateau. Certainly, we've all been around men and women who are godly at a level that is almost embarrassing. We discussed earlier how comparing ourselves to others can go terribly wrong, particularly if we believe our righteousness lies in simply being better than others. It's also dangerous to find ourselves lacking in comparison to others if our aim is simply to be like other people rather than to learn from them about how to love and glorify Jesus. But there is also a holy way to be tutored, mentored, and discipled by other people. We can find good examples, models of Christlikeness, who are strong where we are weak, and whose presence in our lives stretches us and helps us to grow.

When I was in college, I knew a street minister who pretty much lived on the streets, handing out tracts and telling everybody about Jesus. This cat was really out there. I spent some time with him and remember how forthright he was about the gospel. He had zero hang-ups about bringing Jesus into everything.

One of my more vivid memories of time with him was one day when we went out to lunch at Subway. Our time comes to order, and he asks for a six-inch tuna sandwich or something like that. The young woman—excuse me, *sandwich artist*—behind the counter starts making his sandwich, and he asks her very plainly, "Do you think that sandwich could feed five thousand people?"

She replies, "Um, well, no sir. We've got that forty-sub platter for catering. But that's as big as we make them."

He says, "No, no. That sandwich, that sandwich. Do you think that sandwich can feed five thousand people?"

And she says, "Well, no. No, I don't think it could."

Then he says, "Then you don't know my God."

At this point, I'm sort of backing away, thinking, *Hey, I just want my meatball sub.*

I was sort of embarrassed by his evangelistic aggression in the moment. He was just putting it all out there. He didn't think ordering a sandwich was a moment you could detach from the gospel.

This was a good experience for me, a healthy thing. It's a good thing for us to get around people who are beyond us spiritually, particularly in areas where we're weak.

So in my own life I have found that I need to be around pray-ers: people who are good at prayer. I want to be around people whose primary gifting is prayer, people who are passionate about and in prayer. They're going to remind me that I don't need intellect in this practice—I need power.

We all need to surround ourselves with people who have strengths in areas of our weaknesses. Weak in evangelism? Shadow a strong evangelist. Weak in theology? Apprentice with a good studier. Weak in service? Attach yourself to the hospitable, the humble, and the sacrificial.

Never be satisfied with where you are in the area of spiritual growth. Cultivate an insatiability for more of God by examining your weaknesses, beholding the perfection of Christ, and finding good examples of strengths you want to develop.

THE RIGHT DISCONTENTMENT

Not that I have already obtained this or am already perfect, but I press on to make it my own, because Christ Jesus has made me his own. (Phil. 3:12)

I love that Paul, of all people, a man of God at the varsity level of Christian maturity, says here, "I'm still not there." If he can have that holy discontentment at his level of progression, then so can we.

But we have to remember that this is a holy discontentment, which means that this is not dissatisfaction with Christ or our salvation but an ultimate dissatisfaction with ourselves or anything but Christ. This doesn't mean we don't enjoy God's good gifts; it just means we shouldn't seek fulfillment in His gifts at the expense of Him as the Giver.

This is a crucial point. I am not urging here the kind of discontentment that would leave you filled with anxiety, fear, or a constant sense of God's disapproval and frustration with you.

No, I want to encourage instead the type of discontentment that seeks to worship more boldly than we currently do, wants to know more of the Scriptures than we know. This is the type of discontentment that would push us to want to pray more deeply and more powerfully than we do right now.

Likewise, this discontentment is not about getting stuck in a state of immobility. Sometimes we can get so locked into a lack of satisfaction that we just give up, assuming that we will never grow or experience joy. If we dwell in our weaknesses or areas of dysfunction without the framework of the gospel that tells us we are approved of eternally in Christ and totally justified before God, we can get into "analysis paralysis." Instead, the holy discontentment Paul urges is a restlessness that would drive us further and deeper into joy, not away from it. He attacks his own apathy and energy from a few different angles.

I know he says, "One thing I do" (Phil. 3:13), but like any legit preacher, he then lists, like, *five things.* From Philippians 3:13–16, we can identify them like this:

Forget what lies behind.
Strain forward to what lies ahead.
Press on toward the goal.
Think "this way."
Hold true to what you have attained.

That first exercise is crucial to a discontentment that is holy and not sinful or demoralizing. "Forget what lies behind." This forgetfulness cannot refer to everything that is behind us. It can't be a carte-blanche forgetfulness, because over and over in the Scriptures God actually tells His people to *remember.* In the Old Testament, He constantly has them building altars of remembrance. He commands them to remember His past faithfulness to the patriarchs and the patriarchs' past faithfulness to Him. So Paul isn't saying, "Forget everything." In 1 Corinthians 15:1, he even says, "Now I would remind you, brothers, of the gospel I preached to you."

Instead, what he's saying is that he wants to forget anything behind him that might rob him of his pursuit of Jesus Christ. This includes high points as well as low points. Why high points?

We all have victories in our pasts, times when we overcame something trying or depressing. Throughout the Christian life, we experience various "wins." Those wins can all be beautiful reminders of God's provision, of God's power. But they can also make us smug and lazy if we try to rest in those temporary victories. In 1 Corinthians 10:12, Paul actually warns believers about this: "Therefore let anyone who thinks that he stands take heed lest he fall." We need to be most careful about our spiritual state when we are exulting in past victories. Those memories are great, but they are not suitable power for the growth needed today. "Take heed as you stand lest you fall" in this sense means "don't live off the victories of yesterday."

The victory of yesterday was given to you by the grace of yesterday. Today comes with a grace of its own. His mercies are new every morning, like manna delivered to you just in time. Yesterday's grace is inadequate in the face of today's struggle.

But it's not just past victories we need to take heed of—but more obviously, it's past failures. We need to be careful not to let today's pursuit of Jesus Christ be affected by something dark behind us, be it sin or struggle. If it was something bad we did or something bad done to us, we need to take it captive to the obedience of Christ and not let it keep us from seeking Him.

It is so natural and so easy to get bogged down in the idea that what we've done or what we've been through is simply too much for grace to overcome. We declare ourselves untouchable, unreachable, or un-*healable*. Remember Paul's words: "Forget what is behind." Refusing to forget these things, in the end, this is just a subtle form of pride. In doing this we assume that we're the one person who is too much of a problem for Jesus. We're the one nut He can't crack. We've got the one situation for which the cross of Christ is inadequate. *Oh sure, He can save Paul, He can deliver Peter, and He can make all things new. But not me! I've got grace's kryptonite.* And this is how refusing to forget what lies behind is prideful.

On the flip side of that, because of the cross and because salvation is from Christ alone, we can actually come to boast all the more in our dark pasts. No, we do not boast as a way of glorifying sin or championing ourselves, but instead to magnify the wonders of the grace and mercy of Christ. In 1 Timothy 1, Paul does that himself:

> I thank him who has given me strength, Christ Jesus our Lord, because he judged me faithful, appointing me to his service, though formerly I was a blasphemer, persecutor, and insolent opponent. But I received mercy because I had acted ignorantly in unbelief, and the grace of our Lord overflowed for me with the faith and love that are in Christ Jesus. The saying is trustworthy and deserving of full acceptance, that Christ Jesus came into the world to save sinners, of whom I am the foremost. But I received mercy for this reason, that in me, as the foremost, Jesus Christ might display his perfect patience as an example to those who were to believe in him for eternal life. (vv. 12–16)

Elsewhere, he says, "If I must boast, I will boast of the things that show my weakness" (2 Cor. 11:30). It is this fearless exposing of his own inadequacy and sinfulness that prompts Paul to confess in Philippians 3, "Look, I'm not there yet."

But he's not hobbled by the fact that he does not measure up. *He's driven by it.* He can boast in his weaknesses because he knows there is power to be had in the gospel, and in fact, there is only power to be had in the gospel for those who will humbly confess their own weakness. This is another example of the right kind of discontentment at work.

THE FUEL OF GRACE

The right kind of discontentment works. It exerts effort. Because it is not lazy, it does not exist in a state of spiritual stasis but rather in a state of growth. Holy discontentment produces a lot of restless energy that seeks rest in Christ and His gospel. That's where that five-pronged "one thing" of Paul's comes in.

> Brothers, I do not consider that I have made it my own. But one thing I do: forgetting what lies behind and straining forward to what lies ahead, I press on toward the goal for the prize of the upward call of God in Christ Jesus. Let those of us who are mature think this way, and if in anything you think otherwise, God will reveal that also to you. Only let us hold true to what we have attained. (Phil. 3:13–16)

In holy discontentment, we work out what God has worked into us by His Spirit. We do this first by forgetting anything behind us that might rob us of our current pursuit. Then we *move*. Yes, I'm in Christ. Yes, I've found Him. Yes, He's found me. Yes, I belong to Him. Yes, I have Him, but I'm going for more of Him. If there's always more of Jesus to be had, I'm moving. And I'm not just ambling along, aimlessly wandering. I'm straining forward, and I'm pressing onward. I'm pressing on like He's the only prize there is.

Paul loves this kind of language. He uses it all the time:

> Have nothing to do with irreverent, silly myths. Rather train yourself for godliness; for while bodily training is of some value, godliness is of value in every way, as it holds promise for the present life and also for the life to come. The saying is trustworthy and deserving of full acceptance. For to this end we toil and strive, because we have our hope set on the living God, who is the Savior of all people, especially of those who believe. (1 Tim. 4:7–10)

Have nothing to do with irreverent, silly myths. I'll apply this phrase for modern parlance: Don't play games. Don't mess around. Instead, train yourself for godliness. Toil and strive.

Now check out 1 Corinthians 9:23–27:

> I do it all for the sake of the gospel, that I may share with them in its blessings.

> Do you not know that in a race all the run-
> ners run, but only one receives the prize? So run
> that you may obtain it. Every athlete exercises
> self-control in all things. They do it to receive a
> perishable wreath, but we an imperishable. So I
> do not run aimlessly; I do not box as one beat-
> ing the air. But I discipline my body and keep
> it under control, lest after preaching to others I
> myself should be disqualified.

Every time I read that passage I think of the scene in *Rocky II*
when Adrian says to Rocky: "There's one thing I want you to do
for me. Win." And then the music kicks in, and the classic training
montage begins.

Paul is saying that nobody runs a race to lose it. Why would
you run if you're not running to win? So he simply says: run to
win. But he's honest about the fact that you can't do that if you
don't train, if you don't discipline yourself.

It's at this point that some people will bring up the idea of
grace, that revolutionary message at the essence of Christianity,
the truth that makes the biblical faith distinct from every other
religion and means of improvement—and makes it better than all
of them besides. Isn't the idea of grace contrary to this talk about
striving, toiling, training, and disciplining?

One of the best ways to get grace wrong is to believe it means
we don't work in the Christian life. But as Dallas Willard says,
"Grace is not opposed to effort, but to earning."

Nobody stumbles into godliness, ever. It simply doesn't happen. There is no autopilot mode for the Christian life. We never see people in the Bible growing in godliness by coasting along. Not even the person who gets the miracle.

In fact, in the Old Testament we see that when the miracle of God shows up in a profound, amazing way, people eventually start taking it for granted—and when there's no toiling or striving toward holiness, the miracle soon dissipates. Moses goes up on the mountain. He just led the people out of Egypt. While he's up there receiving the Ten Commandments, the people of Israel take out all their gold and make a small calf out of it. And they're making a small calf because people like gods they can control. Then Moses comes down the mountain and sees this abomination. God's power had been on display for these people at a level that none of us have ever seen with our own eyes. He killed the firstborn son of every Egyptian. He turned every bit of water to blood. He parted the Red Sea. He sent infestations of frogs, of locusts. The power of God was on display violently, radically, and visibly. In fact, the reason Moses is up on the mountain by himself is that the mountain shook and the people could hear God in the distance, and they were afraid to go up with Moses. And despite the fact that God revealed His power in such profound ways, in a matter of weeks they're worshipping a golden calf.

Where there's not striving, toil, or pursuit of holiness, power encounters are actually held cheaply. This is why Dietrich Bonhoeffer calls a life of laziness and apathy about the gospel a belief in "cheap grace." Belief in radical grace does not make people turn away from Christ with passion, despite the fact that grace means we are saved apart from how passionate or dispassionate our pursuit is. If we truly believed we were saved apart from our works, we would work harder purely out of gratitude and worship. This is not the same thing as—and should be continually distinguished from—working hard for God's approval. It is the difference between obeying *to be* accepted and obeying because we *are* accepted.

Therefore, it's okay to set spiritual goals. It is good to want to grow in our knowledge of Scripture. And it is not contrary to the work of grace to plan accordingly. In fact, it is quite apropos that grace gets worked out in straining forward and pressing on.

The further into grace we go, the more we will actually understand this. Works are not grace, but works are not incompatible with grace. It was John Calvin who said, "We are saved through faith alone, but not by faith that is alone." Just as God's grace produces our faith, we substantiate our faith by the filling up of works. James 2:26 says this: "For as the body apart from the spirit is dead, so also faith apart from works is dead."

In the end, while some of the high-minded want to pit grace against striving, and while we are not saved *by* our striving and in fact are saved *from* our striving, we are also saved *to* our striving—a striving after Christ. It's not advanced Christianity to avoid the commands of God and the pursuit of holiness; rather, we should seek to understand the dynamic tension between grace and effort. About all that straining and toiling,

Paul writes, "Let those of us who are mature think this way, and if in anything you think otherwise, God will reveal that also to you" (Phil. 3:15).

CHAPTER EIGHT

CENTERING ON
THE GOSPEL

But our citizenship is in heaven. (Phil. 3:20)

Everywhere I go, everybody I meet wants new revelation. I can't think of a better way to put it than that. All of us, most of the time, want to know what's next, what's here, what's now.

Have you seen the television commercial where the guy is having his new big-screen television delivered to his front door, and at that very moment a truck goes by with an advertisement for the newer *new* television? His face drops. We don't want yesterday's technology. And we don't tend to want yesterday's news. The Internet is great at this—or terrible, depending on your perspective. It is so hard to stay ahead of the curve on what's happening, so we log in and never log out. That's why we walk around with our heads down, noses to our phones. We don't want to miss anything.

God forbid we not find out about something hours after it happened. Heaven help us if we have the oldest model of a particular vehicle.

This dynamic takes place in the church, too. By and large we don't want the old stuff. We want new stuff. We want new revelation, which is why, despite the fact that none of us has mastered the Scriptures, we say things like: "God hasn't been talking to me lately." What we mean is: "God isn't giving me the direct hotline of insider info specifically tailored to me."

Our lamenting of God's "silence" while our Bible goes undisturbed is actually quite revealing, because we want new revelation while at the same time we refuse to be obedient to what we already know. We demand to be taught something new.

But it makes no sense to graduate on to an advanced class when we've never cleared the basics. In biblical terms, what we call the basics of Christianity—the gospel of Jesus Christ—is in reality both the beginner's level *and* the advanced class! In the church, I think we often get the milk and the meat confused. We think end-times theories and other theological speculations are the meat, when it's the simple gospel that keeps offering up further depths of wisdom and insight throughout the Christian life. It keeps offering deeper wisdom if we will keep pressing into it.

This is why Paul comes full circle to the gospel at the end of Philippians 3. It's a "check" for us, a pause. It's meant to keep us from getting ahead of ourselves.

Consider this:

Let those of us who are mature think this way,
and if in anything you think otherwise, God will
reveal that also to you. Only let us hold true to
what we have attained. (Phil. 3:15–16)

Paul stops. He puts this check in place in the text. He's basically saying, "Whoa. Before we talk anymore, let's remember what we've already attained. Let's remember that the main thing is the main thing. Let's hold on to what we've been given."

Here we find yet another reminder of the importance of what we might call "gospel-centrality." Why is it important to center on the gospel of Jesus Christ?

First of all, we should keep the gospel ever before our eyes, because we receive Christ in the gospel, and we are told to fix our eyes on Him (Heb. 12:2). It's in beholding Jesus that we are transformed (2 Cor. 3:18), so it makes sense to keep our eyes fixated on Christ.

There's another reason we want to center on the gospel: because the gospel is where we find the power for the Christian life. Romans 1:16, 1 Corinthians 1:17, Ephesians 3:7, and 1 Thessalonians 1:5 all confirm this. Colossians 1 reminds us that the gospel is going forth into the world and bearing fruit. First Corinthians 15 reminds us that the gospel is not just what we received but the power in which we currently stand and by which we continue to be saved. And since we see throughout the New Testament that even our faith is a gift of God's grace and that every imperative of obedience is attached to an indicative of the gospel, we want to stay focused on the gospel so we can follow God. The power to walk by faith in obedience is sourced in the grace of the gospel. So now then: in all our toiling and striving and straining and pressing, "only let us hold true to what we have attained." Or "hold fast," as Paul writes in 1 Corinthians 15:2.

Clearly, centering on the gospel of Jesus is imperative for growth in the Christian life and the passionate pursuit of Jesus. Martin Luther says, "Most necessary it is … that we should know this article well, teach it unto others, and beat it into their heads continually."[1] Or, as Tim Keller says, the gospel is not just the ABCs of the Christian life but the A to Z.

As we conclude the third chapter of Philippians, we see Paul giving us essentially three ways to center on the gospel. These aren't the only means to gospel centrality, of course, but they are three primary and fairly practical ways, things we can implement or bring to mind with good, regular reminders. The three means of gospel centeredness Paul highlights are these: engaging in discipleship, remembering our citizenship, and anticipating heaven.

ENGAGING IN DISCIPLESHIP

Throughout the letter to the Philippians, Paul's been offering examples to follow. We discussed in the previous chapter how living in close proximity with brothers and sisters who are not like us, who are strong in areas where we are weak, can be beneficial to our growth in Christ and our development of a holy discontentment. But here the focus is on modeling, on training. A mark of mature

Christianity is discipleship—making disciples and being discipled. This is where Paul goes in Philippians 3:17: "Brothers, join in imitating me, and keep your eyes on those who walk according to the example you have in us."

Paul is not timid about putting himself out there as an example. But he's not encouraging this so that the church will be full of Paul clones. The best way to take this instruction is found explicitly in 1 Corinthians 11:1: "Be imitators of me, as I am of Christ." Some translations render the verse as, "Follow me as I follow Christ." The implication is that Paul wants people to follow him to the extent that he is teaching them to follow Jesus. They should stop following him if he ceases to lead them to Jesus (Gal. 1:8; Acts 17:11).

This is a paradigm for discipleship. "Join" connotes activity, a connection. You can't be discipled from a distance, in other words. "Imitate me" speaks to the level of training involved. Paul is modeling Christian discipleship, and by "copying" him, in a sense, his own disciples will end up following Christ as well. "Keep your eyes on those who walk according to the example you have in us" means studying the lives—beliefs, customs, habits, temperaments, fruit—of mature Christians in order to learn how to develop their beliefs, customs, habits, temperaments, and fruit.

In a letter to one of his disciples named Titus, Paul spells out a little more how this might look:

> But as for you, teach what accords with sound doctrine. Older men are to be sober-minded, dignified, self-controlled, sound in faith, in love,

and in steadfastness. Older women likewise are to be reverent in behavior, not slanderers or slaves to much wine. They are to teach what is good, and so train the young women to love their husbands and children, to be self-controlled, pure, working at home, kind, and submissive to their own husbands, that the word of God may not be reviled. Likewise, urge the younger men to be self-controlled. Show yourself in all respects to be a model of good works, and in your teaching show integrity, dignity, and sound speech that cannot be condemned, so that an opponent may be put to shame, having nothing evil to say about us. (Titus 2:1–8)

Throughout the New Testament we learn the important reminder that our faith, though personal, was never meant to be private. I have a personal relationship with Jesus Christ. But that personal relationship with Christ was never meant to play out in the privacy of my own mind and heart.

By living out my faith, I become an example to others in following Christ. And when others further along than me boldly live out their faith, they become examples to me. We talk a lot in the church about "sharing our faith" and "being a witness," usually as these practices apply to evangelism. But there is a very real need to continually share our faith with our brothers and sisters, to be witnesses day after day, even to the already converted. We keep evangelizing each other. Indeed, as Dietrich Bonhoeffer says in his book on Christian community, *Life Together*, we should meet each other as bringers of the gospel. We need the word of Christ in each other.

Paul puts himself out there as an example and urges the Philippians to look for other Christians to learn from. We are in no less need of discipleship today. Despite all the information we have in everything from books to blogs, we still need to be trained by living examples, mentors in the faith who will serve us by walking with us. It's our responsibility to find people we can disciple, and it's our responsibility to be discipled.

You and I need to identify godly men and godly women and then put ourselves under their tutelage.

This may be harder for some of us than others. Maybe you actually go to a church or live in an area where mature Christians are somehow hard to come by. I know it happens. I've been in places where I'd hear something like this, and I'd be thinking, *I hear you, Paul. But they're not here.*

Treading lightly here, I still think it falls on us to make an effort to find them.

Maybe you have to travel. Maybe you have to adjust your schedule in inconvenient ways. Discipleship is important enough to make those efforts anyway.

You know, we live in a really great age. Once when my wife and I were headed to lunch, we found that the road we needed to take had been blocked off. So Lauren picked up a phone and hit a button. And the phone told us where to go. She hit a button and it's like, "Take a left right here. Now take a right." Before I knew it, I was eating a really good burger and drinking a peanut butter shake.

With all the ways to connect, all the advances we have in learning and relating, I think it's easier than ever, actually, to find Christians to learn from. It's always best to find Christians you can be in community with, Christians whom you can see regularly up close. Paul says to "keep your eyes on" them (Phil. 3:17). But maybe if you're in a dry place where you're the only Christian in the area, maybe you'll read books by wise men and women, maybe you'll listen to their sermons. Heck, maybe you'll follow them on Twitter! Again, virtual community is no substitute for the intimacy of actual community. You should not make a podcast your pastor or a tweeter your discipler, but these are still valid ways to learn and train and grow.

However you can, identify mature followers who can help you follow Jesus more closely. Get as close to them as you can, as close as they'll let you.

But here's a caution and perhaps a little relief. It might be smart for you to look for Christians who have areas of strength in which you need training and examples. What I mean is, sometimes we hamstring our discipleship process because we're looking for an example in some total package of godliness. And of course those people are often very hard to find. We might be looking for the guy who's fluent in Koine Greek or who has all the end-times charts printed out on his wall. But looking for those guys might be a long and difficult process. Don't think you have to find some perfect Christian to follow.

Don't overlook the "average" Christians around you who may be further along in some areas than you are. Maybe some guy you know isn't the best theologian in the world. But he loves his wife like the Scriptures command. Maybe it's a good idea to get around that guy. Maybe there's a guy who just loves his kids like Jesus commanded him to. Being with him may help you want to love your kids like that and learn how to do it. Maybe you didn't grow up in a healthy home. So maybe you get your theology from some books by dead guys, but you learn how to be a husband and a father at somebody's house.

In any event, one way Paul says to "hold true" to the gospel is to start training in how to apply the gospel to everyday life by engaging in a discipleship relationship.

REMEMBERING YOUR CITIZENSHIP

There's another aspect to our "holding true to what we've already attained" in our passionate pursuit of Christ. It's understanding who we are in Christ.

It's hard for me to remember clearly, but my dad was in the navy and then in the Coast Guard, so we traveled around quite a bit. In the circles we ran in, no one made a big deal of sports. Little League lasted for a season, but when it was over, everyone moved on and played whatever the next sport was in the city leagues. It wasn't like now when you can play soccer year-round and baseball nearly year-round. It just didn't work like that back then.

I played a bit of baseball as a kid but didn't really get into sports until junior high. What I learned very quickly was that I could run really fast in a straight line, but if I tried to move to the left or to the right, tried to turn, tried to stop, tried to do anything else as I ran straight, then things would go bad for me. I would fall over, I would break an arm, or I would trip over a hurdle or something like that. I've joked for years that I had a rare disorder called "uncoordinated lankiness." Basically there seemed to be some sort of disconnect between the brain and the fast-twitch muscle fibers in my body. So while running full speed I would think, *Make a left*, and my body would get confused as to whether I meant right or left and would just freak out and fall over. That was pretty much my athletic background.

I grew up in a predominantly black junior high and played football and basketball. Several of my friends dubbed my style of play "the honky hustle." I'd give it all I had, but usually it didn't go very well. Normally that's not a big deal—even now it isn't a big deal—except that starting out in junior high, you begin to try to figure out who you are by looking around at everybody else. You begin trying to figure out your identity.

You can see this play out by turning on any television program about teenagers, or you can study your own teenagers. They start thinking, *Okay, am I an athlete? Am I a brain?* and, *Which group am I with? Which group am I not with?* There are even these groups that become anti-groups. When I was in high school it was the Goth kids who banded together and were antisocial nonconformists together in the same way.

In adolescence, we all start trying to figure out, *Who am I, and how do I fit into the world?* What usually happens is that we think this search for identity and a group to belong with kind of fades as we go to college, and even more so as we get out of college and enter so-called "real life."

But I don't think that's true.

I think we continue to define and redefine ourselves on a continual basis. We continue to define ourselves through our jobs and where our jobs fall on the socioeconomic scale. We continue to define ourselves by how we're made up physically and emotionally. We continue to define ourselves in these really limited, finite ways.

What I've noticed in Dallas, and I'm sure the same would be true where you live, is that we have people who define themselves by the job they have. These people *are* their job. One of the first questions guys ask each other is, "What do you do?" Because the unspoken assumption is that what you do for a living tells people what, and who, you are.

If we're not careful, we will define ourselves by the houses we live in or by dozens of other external, temporary things. For some people, their entire identity and sense of self-worth are built around their house, their job, their children, their ability to dress in a certain way, or their fitness level. In fact, most fitness regimens have everything to do with vanity and very little to do with actual health. That's why you get the guy doing bicep curls and bench-pressing every day in the gym. It's not like he still needs to go wrestle his dinner to the ground. He just wants to look good at the pool. So it's not really about being in shape; it's about identity.

Every day we communicate, "I want to look this way; I want to be perceived this way," or even, "I want others to be envious of this thing in me," whether that thing is your job, your car, your house, or whatever. So this desire for identity never really goes away; it just changes. It's not "the jocks versus the artsy kids versus the brainy kids" anymore. It evolves into "I'm on the 'upper-middle class, white, drive-a-BMW, have a five-bedroom house with a playroom and an entertainment room' team." Then you've even got the blue-collar egocentric identity, saying, "I'm not some sissy, BMW-driving, caviar-eating, champagne-sipping weenie. I am a genuine Miller Draft, two-dollar hamburger, mac 'n' cheese kind of guy." So you've got pride over on the other side, too, about being *not* the other guy.

What the Bible repeatedly tells us to do, and what Paul shares with us in the final verses of Philippians 3, is to find who we are not in the external but in the internal. Instead of defining ourselves based on what we do or don't do, the gospel would have us remember what Christ has done. Therefore, the Christian's identity is completely built on Him and on nothing else.

When we go outside of Him to determine the substance of our identities, we actually engage in idolatry. In this sense, idolatry says, "I will not be defined by God; I'm going to be defined by other things like my car, my house, etc." You start holding on to those things tightly so that when God wants them, you won't give them up because you think they define who you are. You don't want to let go of your money or live a simpler lifestyle for the good of the kingdom because you've built your identity on those

CENTERING ON THE GOSPEL

things you've accumulated around you. Paul builds the contrast of identities between holding true to the gospel and engaging in idolatry like this:

> For many, of whom I have often told you and now tell you even with tears, walk as enemies of the cross of Christ. Their end is destruction, their god is their belly, and they glory in their shame, with minds set on earthly things. But our citizenship is in heaven. (Phil. 3:18–20)

The idol chasers in this passage are set on earthly things. Their god is their belly. In other words, they do what they want, when they want, how they want. Whatever they feel like doing, whatever feels good, or whatever satisfies temporarily is what they seek *total* satisfaction in.

By contrast, Paul urges the Philippian church to remember the life into which they were called, Him to whom they were united, and the place where their real citizenship rests. In short, he wants to remind them of their identity. If your citizenship is based in the world, it makes sense to live in worldly ways. But if your citizenship is found in heaven, it doesn't make sense to live in worldly ways. In fact, it makes more sense to live as a foreigner or an exile and to find the ways of this consumeristic, materialistic world "alien."

When we live as if this world is all there is, as if all our hope is in stuff that rusts and decays, we are not holding true to the gospel we attained but to treasures that don't last. And so one way to stay focused on the gospel is to remind ourselves constantly of our true citizenship, of our identity. We are people who have been united to Christ. We are hidden with Him in God (Col. 3:3). We are seated with Him in the heavenly places (Eph. 2:6).

Christian, remember your citizenship.

Remember who you are.

Since "doing" flows from "being," and because how we live naturally results from who we know ourselves to be, it is important to think of the gospel in this way at all times. Because of Christ's work, we have been rescued from the idolatry of earthly things. Our God is the one true God, and in Him we have total satisfaction and eternal security.

And it's on that heavenly note that we turn to the third means of daily centering on the gospel.

ANTICIPATING HEAVEN

Paul calls the return of the Lord the "blessed hope" (Titus 2:13). Why? Because he knows that in this difficult life of sin and self-denial, a great reward on the horizon makes a beautiful motivation to passionately pursue Christ. This is exactly where Paul goes at the end of Philippians 3:

> But our citizenship is in heaven, and from it we await a Savior, the Lord Jesus Christ, who will transform our lowly body to be like his glorious

body, by the power that enables him even to subject all things to himself. (vv. 20–21)

Christians, though straining forward, live in a period of waiting. We wait for the return of Jesus Christ. But this is not an idle
waiting. It is a hopeful expectation, and we are called to live as if
this return is imminent, even if it may be a long way off.

D. A. Carson writes:

> Paul insists in the strongest terms that genuine
> Christianity, the kind that he wants imitated,
> lives in the light of Jesus's return. It is the kind of
> Christianity that joins the church in every genera-
> tion in crying, "Amen. Come, Lord Jesus" (Rev.
> 22:20). In short, it is Christianity that is prepar-
> ing for heaven, for that is where our true home is,
> our true citizenship, our true destiny. Only that
> stance is sufficient to make Paul's attitude toward
> suffering sensible and reasonable. If cheerful
> identification with Christ and his sufferings in
> this world finally issues in the spectacular glory
> of the Lord's return and the splendor that follows,
> then we too are vindicated in a fashion somewhat
> analogous to Christ's own vindication.[2]

What Paul wants us to do is live as if the kingdom of heaven
really is at hand like Jesus said it was, as if in some sense it really

was coming to bear in history in and through Him. One way we live like that is to keep our heads up and our imaginations filled with the glories sure to come.

Revelation 15:3 has always fascinated me. People who attend The Village Church know it's a text I talk about all the time. It basically says that in heaven we will sing the song of Moses. I remember first encountering that text and wondering, *Why are we singing about Moses in heaven?* I mean, we don't really even do that at church.

The verse haunted me as I kept trying to figure it out, and I recall how the pieces started to come together. I was reading this story in the gospel of Luke. A woman of the "city" runs into Jesus. He's having dinner with the Pharisees. She busts open the door, and every eye in the room stares at her. She looks around the room and sees Jesus. And before she even gets to Him, she starts to sob. She falls at His feet. She opens up this jar of perfume. And she starts to pour it on His head and on His feet. The disciples and the Pharisees begin to grumble, saying, "If he knew what kind of woman this is, he would never let her touch him."

And Jesus, knowing their thoughts, looks up. He says, "Why do you talk like that? I came in. And you didn't give me a basin. You didn't anoint my head. And you didn't anoint my feet. This woman has done something that is beautiful" (Luke 7:44–48, author's translation).

Here's where Revelation 15:3 starts coming together for me. Jesus says, "Wherever in the world the gospel is preached, the story of this woman will be told" (Mark 14:9, author's translation).

We are roughly two thousand years ahead of that moment now. And I just told you that story like Jesus said I would. The glimpse He gives them—*and us*—is that we live on. We keep going. This world is not the end.

And given the timelessness of the gospel and the timeless joy of heaven, is it so hard to believe that one day when all is said and done—when we're all sitting around the banqueting table of the Lamb, and we've got the new wine in our hands, and we're eating the rich fare of the glorious hereafter, and we're celebrating all that Christ has done—that Moses will stand and hold up his glass in a toast to the Lord and say, "And Christ did this. And He did this. And He did that. And He did this …" On and on and on, recounting the faithfulness of God to him and his generation over and over and over again. And won't the crowd in that moment just blow up? Countless untold billions of us will throw up our hands and cheer, and we'll clink our glasses, raising a ruckus of praise.

Then the great patriarch Abraham will rise to address the multitudes at the feast, and he'll begin to recount God's historic goodness: "And He did this. And He did that. He did that." On and on Abraham will go, telling tales we know and some we don't, but with his first-person recollection and personal joy in God's faithfulness. Then the crowd will blow up again, crying aloud with gladness and uproarious praise. I don't know who I'll sit next to, but I plan on running around and acting as free as I actually am. I plan on giving Calvin a good game, Augustine a big hug, and Bonhoeffer a high five. And we'll all drink up and keep going. And it just keeps on going. On and on down the line. There's no time constraint. We'll sing together the songs of the saints, sharing in this glorious eternal moment about how faithful God was in His grace to broken sinners.

Could it be that the first million years will be filled with just drinking wine and telling these stories?

Maybe this woman—seen on earth through dim eyes as a woman of the night, now in heaven in her glorified state and seen clearly in her identity in Christ—will rise up trembling with cheer, tears of joy (not grief!) in her eyes, to say, "He let me touch His feet. He let me touch His head. And He defended my dignity in front of unjust men."

Is it a stretch to think that we should live for *that day*?

When history as the world knows it no longer exists, and there are no longer any great kings or great wars or great political machinations; when there are no histories of countries left to cherish, no more dollars; when it's no longer the strong versus the weak, and all that's left is the story of the great God and King, and all has been righted, and the heroes are now the missionaries and the ministers of grace—of which every believer can be—and our eyes behold Him as He truly is … *words fail.*

That is where our heart ought to be.

But we are not there. And yet, we are.

Let us wait for that day, expectantly and eagerly. Let us fix our eyes on heaven, where our citizenship is held securely, where we are presently united to Christ in spirit.

Only let us hold true to what we have already attained.

And we will yet attain it.

CHAPTER NINE

REJOICE?

The Lord is at hand. (Phil. 4:5)

Apparently, two ladies in Philippi were having a disagreement. We don't get much background on the nature of the disagreement, but Paul begins the fourth chapter of Philippians by urging them to make amends, to set aside whatever differences they have and seek peace with each other. He calls them out in front of everybody: "I entreat Euodia and I entreat Syntyche to agree in the Lord" (Phil. 4:2).

Why might Paul do this at this point in the letter? He has gone through some serious exposition of the gospel and built his case in love and affection for the passionate pursuit of Christ, the cultivation of holy discontentment, the working out of salvation in grace-driven effort, and the centering on the gospel. After all that, then, he pointedly requests that Euodia and Syntyche put all of that into action by reconciling. He even asks the rest of the church to help them: "Yes, I ask you also, true companion, help these women, who have labored side by side with me in the gospel together with Clement and the rest of my fellow workers, whose names are in the book of life" (Phil. 4:3).

Why would Paul care if everybody's getting along or not?

The primary reason is this: he knows that a divided church is a terrible witness. Where people see in a church anger, dissention, inability to reconcile, and the holding of grudges, they do not see Christ as beautiful. So that would be the biggest reason. But where Paul goes next is rather curious.

Another reason why he would urge the church to put its belief in grace into practice toward unity in fellowship with each other is because he knows that this produces joy. Sticking to our relational guns, holding grudges, giving people what they deserve—all of those things may give us a smug sense of satisfaction. But they cannot produce real, deep, abiding joy.

When the people in a church dwell together in the unity of the gospel and together pursue the building up of one another in love, they are providing fertile soil for the roots of deep joy.

But Paul does not tell them to feel happy. He is not asking them to produce a false feeling. Rather he encourages them to reach an agreement, and then he commands a specific action as a logical response: "Rejoice in the Lord always; again I will say, rejoice" (Phil. 4:4).

It's so important, he commands it twice in the same breath. He tells them (and us) to rejoice again, just in case we missed it the first time or were tempted to gloss over this point.

There are two crucial bits of information in Philippians 4:4 that help us understand this joy Paul commands us to express. The first is this: we are to rejoice "always."

Always?

Yes, always.

Like, when—

Yes, even then.

But what about—

Then, too.

But surely not—

No, even then, as well.

Wait—

ALWAYS?

Yes, always.

Isn't this just a great "churchy" idea? Aren't the outworkings of this command too difficult to be considered reasonable?

One day when my son, Reid, was just a little over one year old, I went home from the office in the middle of the day to surprise my wife for lunch. My wife's a blogger, and she was working on a new post that day.

When I show up, Reid's upstairs napping. Lauren asks me to read what she's written before she posts it, so I sit down to give it a look. And while we're sitting there reading and just catching up, I hear Reid upstairs.

He's not able to get out of his crib yet, of course, but something up there just sounds … wrong. I don't know if you can understand that if you're not a parent, but if you are, you probably know exactly what I'm talking about. You get used to certain sounds of stirring, crying, turning over. You know which silence is normal and which isn't. And this time, something just doesn't sound right.

So I say that.

I say, "What is that?"

Lauren heads upstairs. I sit down at the computer to finish reading her blog post. As I'm scanning through her post, I hear her scream like I've never heard her scream before. She's screaming at the top of her lungs—and she's running down the stairs, carrying my son, who's in a full-on seizure, turning blue and gasping for air. He's trying to breathe, but he can't.

I take Reid from her, set him down on the ground, try talking to him, try to get him to snap out of it, and Lauren starts dialing 9-1-1. The fire department is literally a block from our house, so I hear them, while my wife's on the phone with them, fire up the siren and start the short drive to my house.

I turn Reid on his side. I don't know if he's living or if he's dying, but the ambulance gets there right away, and the paramedics push me out of the way and start working on him. Then they hustle Reid outside and put him in the back of the ambulance.

They turn to Lauren and me and say, "Only one of you can ride in the ambulance."

Now, I don't know how it works in your house, but we didn't even have a discussion about that. We didn't say, "Well, what do you think? Do you want to go?" My wife just gets in the ambulance.

She doesn't even turn around. She doesn't look at me. She doesn't nod. She just gets in the ambulance, and the paramedics tell me, "Follow us."

So I run and get in my car. The paramedics shut the ambulance door. *Boom*, and they're gone. I don't know what hospital they're going to. I quickly start my car and tear off after them, and I keep up with them for maybe about the first mile. They've got a siren, remember, and I don't. So it doesn't take long for me to get cut off and for us to get separated.

I don't know where I'm going. I don't know where they are going. I can't get Lauren to answer her cell phone. And I don't know if my one-year-old son is about to die.

How do you rejoice then? Because God is *not* saying through Paul, "Rejoice when everything's going well." He said, "Rejoice always." "Always" includes when they put your son in the back of an ambulance. Or when you get put in there yourself.

Rejoice in the Lord. Always. And again I say, rejoice.

We need help then, don't we? I want to rejoice always, but I need help on the day I'm stuck at a stoplight, my son and wife are gone, I have no idea where to go, I don't know if he's going to make it—how in the world could I possibly rejoice? Because as out-of-the-normal as those situations are for many of us, they are still real-life situations, right? Maybe not everyday situations, but this is real-life stuff. Nearly every one of us has had an emergency moment, perhaps several.

Every one of us knows that our whole world can unhinge with one phone call. Everything we understand about life and everything we take for granted as normal can change in a second.

How do we rejoice in those moments?

Thank God that He tells us. He doesn't leave us hanging.

A TOTALLY REASONABLE JOY

Mature believers in Christ rejoice in the Lord always. Just as Paul surprises us by connecting the conflict between Euodia and Syntyche with rejoicing, he surprises us by connecting rejoicing always—even in the midst of suffering and intense difficulty, perhaps even death—with … *reasonableness*?

Yes. He writes, "Let your reasonableness be known to everyone" (Phil. 4:5).

Well, okay, but now I still need help. Because if you're appealing to *reasonableness* on the day that I can't find the ambulance carrying my son to the hospital, I have to confess that it's a little hard to come by. I'm not acting reasonably in that moment. I'm freaking out. I'm inwardly collapsing. In the chaos and the fear and the sheer panic of the moment, I don't have any reasonableness in me.

However, this reasonableness, or gentleness in some translations, is not built on or predicated by my circumstances. It never is. That's why Paul is able to say, "Rejoice in the Lord always." The reasonableness he wants us to be known for is built on the next group of words in the text. The train of thought goes like this:

"Let your reasonableness be known to everyone" (4:5).

Why?

Because "the Lord is at hand" (4:5).

Why do the mature rejoice in the Lord always? They can be reasonable in the midst of whatever situation they find themselves in precisely because the Lord is always at hand.

The basis of this is doctrinal. The essence of this is spiritual. When you put those two things together, you come up with doxology. That word *doxology* basically comes from two Greek words—*doxa*, which means belief, and *logos*, which means word(s). Literally, *doxology* means "words of belief," but the way in which it is used is as confessional praise, or an expression of worship. In the New Testament, the Greek word *doxa* becomes somewhat synonymous with "glory" as well. So a doxology, like what you might sing at the end of your church worship service, is an ascription of glory to God in a song of praise that expresses a doctrinal truth. The most famous doxology, often called simply "The Doxology," goes like this:

> *Praise God from whom all blessings flow*
> *Praise Him all creatures here below*
> *Praise Him above ye heavenly host*
> *Praise Father, Son, and Holy Ghost.*
> *Amen.*

This doxology is an expression of praise that communicates important doctrinal truths about God: He is the source of all blessings, He is the creator of all creatures, and He is a Trinity.

We find doxologies like this in the Bible as well—Romans 11:33–36 is an example—and it should come as no surprise that as Paul gets worked up in outlining the depths of theological truths revealed to him by the Holy Spirit, he erupts in praise. This is the purpose of theology, in any event: *worship*. If our theology does not drive us to worship God in Christ, it is pointless.

In Jeremiah 32, the prophet Jeremiah is in prison. I always like to talk about or write about people in prison or people about to die just so you'll know that following Jesus doesn't always end up with you being wealthy and healthy and everyone loving you. There's a bit of that out there today, and I just want to continually point out that actually, in the Bible, it rarely, if ever, works that way. So here's one of those cases. Jeremiah, like Paul centuries later, says everything God wants him to say. He has been obedient to all God asked him to do, and he finds himself imprisoned by his own countrymen. The Chaldeans are about to overthrow Jerusalem.

So Jeremiah says, "Repent. Turn to the Lord, or the Chaldeans will burn this place to the ground." He rebukes and proclaims, over and over. The leaders of Israel get tired of him, so they put him in prison.

Faithful Jeremiah is in prison, and the Chaldeans are at the wall. It's almost over, and when it's all said and done Jeremiah gets to go into captivity with the people who imprisoned him, those who didn't heed his call to repent and see the city saved.

Now, let's look at what Jeremiah says in 32:17: "Ah, Lord GOD! It is you who have made the heavens and the earth by your great power and by your outstretched arm! Nothing is too hard for you."

Look at the spirit inside of a man who's in a horrific place—but whose eyes are on God and not on his circumstances. This is a man who is in a far more difficult spot than nearly all of us right now, and his eyes are on God, not on himself. What's his response? He sings: "Ah, Maker of the heavens and earth! Nothing is too hard for you." He's exulting! He's erupting in doxology, poetic words of belief.

Where is his confidence coming from? Clearly it is not coming from his surroundings or his predicament. He trusts in the sovereign power and holy justice of the loving Lord God. The prophet goes on to say:

> You show steadfast love to thousands, but you repay the guilt of fathers to their children after them, O great and mighty God, whose name is the LORD of hosts, great in counsel and mighty in deed, whose eyes are open to all the ways of the children of man, rewarding each one according to his ways and according to the fruit of his deeds. You have shown signs and wonders in the land of Egypt, and to this day in Israel and among all mankind, and have made a name for yourself, as at this day. You brought your people Israel out of the land of Egypt with signs and wonders, with a strong hand and outstretched arm, and with great terror. And you gave them this land, which you swore to their fathers to

give them, a land flowing with milk and honey.
(Jer. 32:18–22)

Jeremiah's exultation is in the exaltation of God. He is ascribing all power and authority and dominion to God. The Israelites
may have imprisoned Jeremiah, and the Chaldeans might be about
to take him captive, but God is on His throne, so everything is
under sovereign control. Jeremiah acknowledges that there is nothing anywhere in the universe that God doesn't rightly stand over,
reign over, and rightly proclaim as "Mine." Everything's His.

Since everything is God's, if God wants something, what could
you possibly do to stop Him from getting it? For instance, if He
wants your life, what are you going to do, eat spinach and go to
pilates? Go ahead—good luck with that. All you have to do is hop
online, and you can find somewhere in the world a guy who died
today even though he ran marathons and never ate anything but
chicken and vegetables. And he was in his thirties. So, yeah, good
luck wagering your invincibility on the paleo diet.

It's all His.

My favorite verse in the Bible that speaks to this is actually
not the "cattle on a thousand hills" reference (Ps. 50:10), mostly
because I'm more of a city guy and, well, cattle scare me. Instead, I
like Deuteronomy 10:14: "Behold, to the LORD your God belong
heaven and the heaven of heavens, the earth with all that is in it."

I've always loved that verse, because if you've ever seen the
Hubble telescope's pictures of all those beautiful clusters, you can
sort of visualize how this text is saying, "The skylines on those

planets? Those are His too. The heavens and the heavens of the heavens. And the heavens of those heavens. Those are all His."

He is infinitely wealthy.

And then I think about this: not only is everything that exists His, but He can make more of anything out of nothing anytime He wants. And He sustains it all by His power.

In fact, Jeremiah says that God actually breathed the stars out. How did the stars get into the heavens? God breathed. *His breath.* So the stars continually call our attention back to God's "Godness" in creation. I don't know what you read or what you dial into, but do you know that if the earth were spinning just a few miles an hour faster or slower, then life as we know it would be impossible? If the sun's temperature were different in either direction, life on this planet would be next to impossible.

Do you realize the billions and trillions of things that have to be governed in order for life to be sustained in any way? Do you know how complex you are as an individual person? Scientists and doctors and people who look at the human body are constantly baffled at what the human body can do. So that's why you get statistics and bell curves, because ultimately doctors and scientists are guessing based on the data they have. They're guessing based on a swath of people. How is that possible? They get to cut people open, right? This isn't the 1400s or 1500s. Scientists and doctors are allowed to study the human body without any guilt or shame, without any kind of religious "that shouldn't happen." Today, they have total freedom to explore and to watch how the human body operates.

However, that human body continually operates in such a way that makes the experts go, "That doesn't make any sense. That shouldn't be happening." Ask a doctor the next time you're in his or her office how much is mystery. Now, a doctor is very educated, very able to guess, but sometimes the body does stuff that doesn't make sense. So that's just a body, one body. Not the universe! Not ecosystems and what's necessary for an ecosystem to thrive and flourish. Not the ocean and why it's salty. All these little things are God's Godness made visible in creation.

The Bible describes your life and mine like this: you're there in the morning, and you're gone by midmorning. That's how God describes the longevity of our lives: a vapor. And I'm going to scrutinize the God of all creation?

But that's not the only place we see God's Godness. We also see God's Godness in *providence*. When I talk about providence, what I'm talking about is the reign and rule of God over details.

Once, my wife was scheduled to fly out early on a Saturday morning to speak at a conference in Orlando. So we get up early, get her to the airport early, drop her off, and I head home to take care of the kids. But then I get this call from Lauren. At first, I think she's calling to tell me she's on the plane, to say, "I'll call you when I land." But she is just in tears. I'm not going to drop any airline's name, but you know who you are.

She doesn't make her flight. She's checked her bag. Bag is on the plane. Bag actually gets to go to Orlando. But my wife is scheduled to speak to several thousand women in Orlando and instead is now on standby. The airline in question has overbooked all their flights to Orlando that day by at least seven people. She becomes number forty on the standby list. The airline starts offering five-hundred-dollar vouchers to people who are willing to give up their seats. I decide to call the airline people to see what I can do. I'm just trying to get her on the plane. They say, "She's not making it to Orlando. We're sorry, Mr. Chandler."

So my wife is crying. And it's that kind of crying rage where you're not really sure how to help. *Should I comfort? Should I enter? Should I not? Should I just give her space?* It feels like a life-and-death kind of scenario. So she's crying, but she's angry, and she's at the gate. The woman at the gate asks my wife, "Is everything okay?" So Lauren says, "Well, I was supposed to go to this conference in Orlando. They're expecting me. I was going to speak on God being the stability of our times"—which, you know, was just perfect—"but I'm not going to make it now. I know I'm not going to make it. My husband just called. He said I wasn't going to make it. He's on his way to pick me up, and I'm just heartbroken. I really felt like the Lord wanted me there."

So this woman asks Lauren to share the talk with her. Lauren starts telling her that God will be the stability of our times, and she shares our story and about how God has been so faithful. This woman tears up because she has felt abandoned by God and a bit lost in life. God reveals His love to this woman at Gate A26.

That's providence! In what was our moment of being stuck, frustrated, and disappointed, God orchestrated a moment in which to reveal His love for this woman.

> The word of the LORD came to Jeremiah: "Behold,
> I am the LORD, the God of all flesh. Is anything
> too hard for me?" (Jer. 32:26–27)

That day when the ambulance disappeared out of my sight, knowing that God is God—that nothing is too difficult for Him, that His love and His sovereignty are real—was my foundation. When my heart and mind wanted to go to every plausible reason why despair made sense, the fact that nothing is too hard for God became my reason, my rationality.

This is why the mature Christian is reasonable. Because, as Paul says, "the Lord is near," even in a desperate situation like the one I described. Because in that moment, here's what I had at the ready: the knowledge that the God of the universe, the God who rescued and saved me, is not Himself powerless at all in that moment, is not at all surprised or shocked by that moment, is not reeling one bit or trying to figure out what to do in that moment. The God of the Bible is not an ambulance driver who shows up after the wreck and hops out and thinks, *Okay, let's do some triage here*. The God of the Bible does not show up after the accident and try to fix it. That's not what He does.

He's there. He knows.

And on that day, the Lord was near, and my son's life was not too difficult for Him to save. He could be trusted with my son. Reid was and is His. My wife is His. My daughters are His. I am His.

My prayer, then, is, "Lord, help me rejoice in You in this moment. Because I know You are in control. I know You love me;

I know You love my family. And I don't understand what You're doing, and I don't know how things are going to work out. But help me to acknowledge that if I have You, I have everything."

My prayer in that moment, seeking joy in all circumstances, is similar to Job's—"Though he slay me, I will hope in him" (Job 13:15)—and Jehosephat's—"We do not know what to do, but our eyes are on you" (2 Chron. 20:12).

Now, let me be very clear, because I'm not trying to make this whole exercise stupid. I didn't sit in my car with an idiot grin on my face, saying, "Well, I'm glad the Lord's here, and this is great! Rejoice in the Lord always; and again, I say rejoice!"

That wasn't happening. That's what we might call an unreasonable theology. God is not glorified when you act happy about horrific things.

He's glorified when, in the deepest possible pain you experience, you still find a way to say, "I trust You. Help me, because my heart is failing in my chest. Help me! My son is Yours. His soul is Yours. His life is Yours. You loaned him to me for Your good to begin with. And I know I'm supposed to hold him loosely, and if you take him home, he's Yours ... but I'd like to keep him."

My friend Jud Wilhite reminds us that we have to sometimes fight for joy:

> For some Christians, it is easy to find joy. For many others, finding happiness or joy is a herculean effort. If you are torn, fight tooth and nail for joy in God. The Bible indicates that joy is

something we choose as much as it is something that happens to us. The Scriptures command us to rejoice throughout. One example is Paul's urging in the emphatic Philippians 4:4....

But how do we do that? When the world seems to be crumbling around us, how do we choose joy? Still more, how are we to "be full"? It sounds as though the command is to do something that happens to us, to be active about something that is essentially passive. How is that possible?

You can experience this filling by simply remaining open to the work of God. Only the Spirit can make your joy full, but you can stay open to this filling by creating conditions in your life that are best used by the Spirit.[1]

In the middle of pain and suffering, of stress and terror, I want to say to God, "Show me what You want to do in this situation." I want to trust. And trust is something we can still do in the middle of our devastation.

This is what gives me reasonable faculties, knowing that the God of the universe does not show up late and is not out of control. Instead, He's in the car with me, and He's in the ambulance with Reid—and so rejoice; and again I say, rejoice!

In the end, all turned out well with my son. But in those moments when joy is hard to come by, I go back to that painful, desperate day. And I use my imagination like this: I see the Lord in that ambulance with my son. I see the Lord caring for my wife, calming my wife, and giving peace to my wife. I see His glory filling that ambulance with infinite power. Regardless of how it might have ended, I see God as fully in control and fully loving in that moment.

And that is my hope for you.

I'm no stranger to loss and sorrow. I know that many reading this book even now barely have the strength to hold it. My hope is that God might redeem some of those things that have wounded you. Perhaps you're thinking of them right now. Maybe you need to ask Him to redeem some of those situations where you felt like He abandoned you. Maybe you want to offer up to Him some of your pain and doubt right now, in this very moment: "[Cast] all your anxieties on him, because he cares for you" (1 Peter 5:7).

It is totally reasonable to do this.

CHAPTER TEN

NO WORRIES

What you have learned and received and heard
and seen in me—practice these things, and the
God of peace will be with you. (Phil. 4:9)

When I first arrived at The Village Church, it was called Highland Village First Baptist Church, and man, did we have some work to do. I don't know how else to say it. The people there loved the Lord, wanted to see people saved, and wanted the church to grow in width and depth. Even with this desire in place, though, we had some work to do, and God started doing some great things immediately. One of our first colleagues in the work of revitalization was a man at the church named Dell Steel, who was in his late sixties.

Right away, I committed to what I *wasn't* going to do. I wasn't going to come into this declining church with its aging membership and say, "Old people, be quiet and get out of our way! There's a new guy in town." I just think that's a really dumb way of trying to reengage a dying church. So I sat down with Dell in one of those early days and just said, "Hey, brother, I need you. Please, can you help us? Can you help me?"

And Dell looked across the table and said, "If you'll preach the Word and men get saved, I don't care what you do. Change whatever you need."

So we did. We preached the Word. God saved people. And we changed the music. We put old, ineffective programs out to pasture and started new initiatives. We moved to establish a plurality of elders for our church governance, and Dell became the chairman of our elder board.

I will never forget that one night near the end of an elder meeting when he said, "Hey, I'm having some problems. I've got to go to the doctor. I've got to get this thing checked out." Soon after, I met with him and a few other men at the church for prayer. He told me they had found out that he had cancer, and, while there really is no such thing as a "good" kind of cancer, it was a particularly bad kind. It wasn't the type that you beat. He said that maybe they could buy him some time, but barring a miracle, he'd been handed a death sentence.

I walked with Dell from that moment of the bad news through his chemo, through his radiation, through the doctor's visits, through the prayers and the tears, all the way to the hospital room and into the moment the Lord called him home. And here is what filled his mind and his heart every step of the way: the peace of God that passes all understanding. That's what marked him. Not anxiety for his wife, not anxiety for his children and his grandchildren, not anxiety for me, not anxiety for the church, not a bit of stress about anything else. *He knew.* We talked about this. I got to watch it unfold. I got to watch a man die well, filled with the peace of God that passes all understanding.

Can you agree with me that the natural man doesn't want to die? The natural man wants to war against death. The natural man is fearful about what might come next. The natural man is fearful about what might happen to his wife, what might happen to his kids. The natural man, as he feels himself wasting away, worries about his exit from the world and is overwhelmed with questions about what happens next—to him and to those he leaves behind.

Dell did not die like that. He thought, *If God wants to save me, He can. And if God wants to take me home, let's go home.* It always blew my mind that he could be so calm about the whole thing, just so straightforwardly peaceful. A good description for the way he suffered might be "resolutely peaceful."

Joe Thorn writes about "suffering well," showing us the foundations of resolute peace:

> God does not promise to rid your life of affliction
> and difficulty. He does, however, offer to give you
> the grace needed to suffer well, and through grace
> to discover the riches and beauty of the gospel.
> It isn't wrong to ask God to relieve you of your
> pain, but it is more important that in the midst of
> the pain you rely on the promise of God to work

such experiences for his glory and your good—to use these times as a means of perfecting your faith, strengthening your spirit, and transforming your life in such a way that you are becoming more like Jesus.[1]

Becoming like Jesus, yes. We become like Jesus in His suffering by sharing in His suffering through our own suffering. We become like Jesus by faithfully holding Jesus as our supreme treasure, joy, and hope. My friend Dell exemplified this faithfulness in his suffering and death. He took Philippians 1:21 and put skin on it: "To live is Christ, and to die is gain."

NO WORRIES

Mature faith, remember, is always rejoicing. Philippians 4:4–5 is actually a great segue into Philippians 4:6 because the unequivocal command to rejoice complements the nonnegotiable about worry. Paul writes, "Do not be anxious about anything" (v. 6). This connection makes sense, because if we are busy rejoicing, we won't have the time to be anxious.

The larger context of Philippians asks the rhetorical question, "What would you have to be anxious about?" There is not a square inch of creation in which God isn't present and sovereign. If we could get out of our heads the idea that the future is something God simply knows and get into our heads the idea that the future is a place where God already *is*, that He doesn't just know about the past and see the present and know about the future, but that He stands outside of time and reigns over all of it sovereignly, what would we have to be anxious about?

If you will be honest about your life, you will admit that God has never failed you. He has never let you down. He may not have always given you what you wanted or orchestrated your life according to your desires or taken your advisement on His providential care for you, but when it comes down to it, He has never, ever failed you. You may have felt distant from God at times, but He's never abandoned you. He has never left you or forsaken you. You have never been without His love and sovereign care.

So even if that phone rings and the worst possible news is on the other end, what do you have to be anxious about?

I understand fear. I understand pain. But that's not the same as worry. Fear is legitimate for the vulnerable, and pain is a natural consequence of being mortal. But worry is a choice made in distrust. And it never helps. Worry contributes nothing to the problems we're facing. "Do not be anxious about anything." Here is the logic of Jesus on the subject: "Which of you by being anxious can add a single hour to his span of life?" (Matt. 6:27).

But it's so hard not to be anxious. I know I shouldn't be anxious, but I feel anxious plenty of times. Like those moments when I'm traveling by plane and I suddenly realize that there's nothing underneath me. Sometimes right in the middle of the flight, I'm thinking, *Wow, we're in the sky*. It's hard not to be anxious. I have daughters, okay? I hate all the boys now. I see them as punks—little shady punks. Can we just be honest that it's hard not to be anxious about certain things? It's hard not to have legitimate anxieties in your heart.

Michael Kelley's two-year-old son, Joshua, was diagnosed with leukemia in 2006. Michael chronicles his family's journey of faith through Joshua's illness and treatment in the book *Wednesdays Were Pretty Normal,* in which he writes this about anxiety:

> I was a worried father, and I felt bad about that. Christians aren't supposed to worry; it's bad form. Jesus tells us not to worry about stuff like clothes or food because we have a foundation of trust in God as our provider.
>
> Paul elaborated on the Christian response to worry in Philippians 4:6 saying: "Don't worry about anything, but in everything, through prayer and petition with thanksgiving, let your requests be made known to God." … That doesn't mean I couldn't rationalize my own worry.
>
> After all, we had plenty to worry about. And one could make the argument that there's a thin line between being anxious and being prepared. Don't responsibility and worry sort of hold hands? Shouldn't we plan for retirement? Shouldn't we have life insurance? Shouldn't we think about the future? Where do you draw the line between responsibility and anxiety? And while we're at it,

why would God be so concerned about His kids' anxiety?…

When we live with a lack of anxiety about the future, even in those tightrope kind of times, we communicate the truth that our God is indeed worthy of our trust. We don't fret over the future because He holds it in His hands. We don't wring our hands in worry because we know He's charting the course. That sort of confidence invites others into it, those longing for something different from life without a net.[2]

Michael's words certainly remind us of the necessary engagement of faith in community and the needs to disciple, be discipled, and look for other worthy Christians to emulate. Anxious Christians are bad advertisements for the God of all comfort.

But "not being anxious" doesn't come without the sweat of faith. Fortunately Paul goes on to show us the antidote for anxiety.

WORRY AT GOD

How does the mature believer handle anxiety? Paul has already told us to remember that "the Lord is at hand" (Phil. 4:5). That's the first and most important step. God is right there, right beside you. You are united with Christ in faith, so you enjoy mystical union with Him. The Holy Spirit dwells in you, so you enjoy constant communion with Him. The Father is not far from any of us (Acts 17:27), and we know that He's especially near to the brokenhearted (Ps. 34:18). Therefore, the omnipresence of God in unfailing love is a tremendous encouragement and ample ammunition against bouts of anxiety.

But how do we engage in the reality of God's presence? This is what Paul says the mature Christian does instead of worrying: "Do not be anxious about anything, but in everything by prayer and supplication with thanksgiving let your requests be made known to God" (Phil. 4:6).

Prayer is the discipline. We take our anxieties to God. Paul even categorizes the kind of prayer for us: *supplication*. So the discipline that we combat anxiety with is the discipline of supplication. Supplication prayers are "help me!" prayers.

We're starting to come full circle now, aren't we? We began our walk through Philippians with the encouragement toward lowliness, humility, and reverent awe of God. This is the posture of supplication. "Help me, Lord! Have mercy on me, Lord!"

Really, prayer and worry are of the same essence. They are both a rehearsing of circumstances, a mulling over, and a kind of mental and emotional chewing. But in worry, there's no connection, no traction, no relational receiver. It's like spinning our wheels. Worrying is like trying to travel in a rocking chair.

But when we pray, we are "worrying" at God. We take those anxieties and direct them Godward, taking them to Him, placing them before Him, and—of utmost importance—handing them over. This is why Martin Luther says, "Pray, and let God worry."

We have a supreme example of this supplication in the prayer of Jesus in the garden of Gethsemane. Facing His impending arrest, torture, and execution, Jesus is so grieved and broken that He is sweating blood as He prays. The God-Man trembles, fears, and makes supplication. He prays, "My Father, if it be possible, let this cup pass from me," but then adds, "nevertheless, not as I will, but as you will" (Matt. 26:39). What has Jesus done? He has obeyed the command not to worry by worrying at God. He takes His anxiety to the Father and hands it over.

However, supplication is not the only quality of anxiety-attacking prayer.

WORRY'S KRYPTONITE

Paul says that our supplication to God should be accompanied "with thanksgiving." This thanksgiving is a sort of humble, "Thank You, Lord, for hearing me." It is a thankfulness for God's listening ear and caring heart.

This thankfulness should be a part of our prayers regardless of whether He answers the way we want Him to. In the terror of our episode with Reid, it would not have been supplication with thanksgiving if we'd reserved our thanks until we found out how the whole thing was going to end, or until we could see whether Reid survived. Of course, we are forever thankful that Reid survived! But the true test of the maturity of our faith would be whether we were prepared to engage in thanksgiving if it had ended terribly. Could we enter God's presence with

175

thanksgiving and His courts with praise, even if He had taken away our son?

This is not about being thankful for the loss. It is about being thankful for having had the gift. It's about remembering that God is good and that He does good. That He gives and takes away and at all times His name is and should be blessed.

"In everything by prayer and supplication with thanksgiving let your requests be made known to God" (Phil. 4:6). In everything, Paul says.

So we fill up the space where anxiety grows with humble, lowly "help me" prayers that are full of thanksgiving for God's goodness, God's gifts, and the ultimate good gift, the gospel. The gospel is grounds for unassailable joy. If the gospel is true, it puts eternal stability into the hearts of all who believe it. And it is a wellspring of "in everything" thanksgivings.

Thanksgiving and worry can't occupy the same space. Thanksgiving is worry's kryptonite. You can't worry if you're giving thanks.

When we go to God with our supplication and thanksgiving, our worry and anxiety flee like roaches when the lights come on. Something else takes their place: "And the peace of God, which surpasses all understanding, will guard your hearts and your minds in Christ Jesus" (Phil. 4:7).

Paul now switches from the emotive state of the believer into the mental state. In doing so, he shows us how you can't separate the two states. Oh, lots of people want to try. We divide ourselves so often between the feelers and the thinkers.

The feelers will say things like, "Why can't we just love? Why do we have to do all this doctrine stuff? Let's just love Jesus." They sometimes look at people who care about doctrine as cold, as numb, as though they'd be more spiritual "if only they just felt what we feel."

At the same time, the more intellectual thinkers look with suspicion at those who emphasize love. They may criticize the feelers by saying, "Oh, how ridiculous and shallow and weak. They need more theology in their smoothie."

What ends up happening is the forming of rival factions that ought to be complementing each other and working together in unity. But instead they both end up acting with arrogance and ignorance because, while God loves an innocent, beautiful heart that loves Him completely, this reality does not negate the fact that we should love Him *correctly*.

Imagine if I were to go home at the end of the day to see my wife. What if I am just overtaken by her beauty, her gorgeousness, and I just kneel right on the floor before her and say, "Baby, I love you so much right now my heart hurts. I don't just love you; I am in love with you. And I don't know if it's your black hair or your brown eyes or what—just the sight of you is *wow*."

Some of you might be thinking, *That's so sweet!*

But let me explain. Let me tell you why, if I were to do that, it would go very badly for me. My wife has blonde hair and blue eyes. Even if my emotions were powerful and appropriate, my wife is going to have a problem with how I expressed them.

Love is not simply something that we feel. It encompasses our affections, yes. It gets expressed in emotional ways, yes. But the Bible tells us that real love "rejoices with the truth" (1 Cor. 13:6). I assume from Ephesians 4:15 that it's possible to speak the truth from a lack of love, and by extension, that it's possible to express love from a place of ignorance and even falsehood. But mature, godly love is a truthful, orthodox, doctrinal love. It brings the thinking and feeling together as Paul does in Philippians 4:7 when he says that the surpassing peace of God will guard our minds *and* our hearts.

If your mind doesn't stir up genuine affection, then I think you're in a lot of danger. The mind and heart feed each other. John Piper says that the intellect exists to throw logs into the furnace of our affections for God. And because Paul is anything but unhelpful, he immediately gives us instructions on how to guard our minds in Christ Jesus. He tells us exactly how to regulate our minds so that we can continue to throw logs into the furnace of our affections for God.

WORRY ON THESE THINGS

Finally, brothers, whatever is true, whatever is honorable, whatever is just, whatever is pure, whatever is lovely, whatever is commendable, if there is any excellence, if there is anything worthy of praise, think about these things. (Phil. 4:8)

I use the word *worry* here because the function is the same, although the focus and the results are different. When we are anxious, we dwell on the negative in a way that demonstrates a lack of trust in God. In this sense, worry wastes mental time. Instead, Paul says, mentally chew on these things.

In our minds, we must constantly operate in the truth, taking "every thought captive to obey Christ" (2 Cor. 10:5). We will think on, dwell on, and buy into what is true, and we will rebuke and flee from what's not true. So then, part of having the mind of a mature believer is being able to spot lies and embrace the truth. It is learning the practice of discernment and maintaining a commitment to growing in biblical wisdom.

Most of us fall into sin because we buy into a lie and walk according to that lie instead of being able to readily identify, "That's not true. *This* is true."

Paul also tells us to mentally dwell on whatever is honorable as opposed to what is dishonorable. I don't want to get scattered in the imaginations of a prideful heart, so I work up in my imagination a celebration of that which has honor, dignity, and the glory of God about it.

Let me give you an example of dwelling on what's honorable. I don't know God's plan for my life in regards to the number of days He's given me. Since my cancer diagnosis, I have lived with a more ready awareness that my life is a vapor. But it doesn't have to be cancer that takes me out. I could die tomorrow in a car crash or freak accident or a variety of other ways. I have no idea what God has in store for me, but here's a little thing I have in my mind. Should He grant me longevity, I want to, when I am seventy or eighty years old, still get up in the morning, drink a cup of coffee with Lauren, hear about the crazy dreams she had the night before, and enjoy the morning with her and the Word of God. We're just a couple of old lovers who've put a lot of time in. And we're drinking coffee and talking about our grandbabies who have come to know the Lord.

That's a fantasy of mine, and this is what I do with it: when in the normal flow of life I see an attractive woman, and that attractive woman is flirtatious; when I am tempted to be lazy when it comes to going after my children's hearts—because it's one thing to be a present father and another thing to go after your children's hearts; when I am tempted to dwell on all kinds of dishonorable things, I go back to that fantasy: me at eighty, drinking a strong cup of coffee on the back porch, talking with my wife about the salvation of our grandchildren. That's something honorable worth dwelling on. And when we dwell on thoughts like that, peace begins to fill our minds. And our hearts.

Sometimes in the life of the mind, you battle image with image. To get one dishonorable image out of your head, you have to replace it with an honorable one. You can't battle it with nothing, right?

Whatever is true and whatever is honorable, dwell on these things.

The same holds true for whatever is just, pure, lovely, commendable, excellent, and praiseworthy. What Paul would have us know is that these virtues find their apotheosis in Christ Himself. We are not meant to simply park our minds around ethereal virtues and "good ideas" but rather to set our minds on things that come from Christ, commend Christ, and consummate in Christ. This is why Paul bookends this mental and emotional "mulling" with references to these qualities' divine personification. In Philippians 4:7 he says that God's peace will guard our hearts and minds "in Christ Jesus." Then, after going through the list of virtues to "worry" on, he says in Philippians 4:9 that "the God of peace will be with you."

Commenting on this passage, John Phillips writes:

> Paul was challenging us to "think on"—think out, take account of—things that are true, honorable, just, pure, lovely, and of good report. And where will such thoughts lead us? To Jesus! In Him all these abstracts are translated into a warm and wonderful personality, a noble and inspiring person.
>
> We cannot think of Christ ever being anything but true. We cannot conceive of Him telling a lie or being deceitful or underhanded. We cannot think of Him being anything less than honorable. With David Livingstone, we think of Him as "a Gentlemen [sic] of the strictest and most sacred honor." On this earth Christ was always just and fair, whether dealing with a fallen woman or a self-righteous Pharisee. How lovely He was! …
>
> Before laying the choices and challenge of Philippians 4:8 before us, Paul penned two words at the end of verse 7: "Christ Jesus." Verse 8 stems

directly out of thoughts of Jesus and leads us directly back to thoughts of Jesus. We must think of Christ. That is the ultimate secret of a positive thought life. All unworthy thoughts perish in His presence.[3]

The mature man or woman—no, let's call him or her the *maturing* man or woman, because that person isn't done yet—is going to have a heart that can rejoice in any circumstance because he or she understands that the Lord is near and understands who the Lord is, and this information makes it reasonable even in the most catastrophic of circumstances to have hope, experience joy, and choose thanksgiving. Maturing men and women, when tempted to fall prey to anxiety, go to the Lord, humble themselves, and hand their anxieties over, trusting Him to answer however He sovereignly sees fit. In their minds, they constantly dwell on what is true, right, honorable, excellent, just, and lovely—mind and heart in sync, maturing unto the Lord.

Paul concludes these thoughts with the third iteration of something we've seen him say before: "What you have learned and received and heard and seen in me—practice these things, and the God of peace will be with you" (Phil. 4:9).

Philippians is an interesting book because Paul really does keep saying the same thing over and over and over. Specifically, rejoicing, humility, and maturity are recurring ideas in this book. And Paul says one more time in verse 9 what he's been saying throughout the letter: "Practice these things."

The fact that he has to tell us to practice—to strain, to press, to "work out"—tells us again that this stuff doesn't happen naturally. These things happen by the power of the Holy Spirit, of course, working through the gospel, but they don't just come out of our natural state by accident.

It's not natural to rejoice in all things. Instead it's natural, isn't it, to feel like you got robbed, to feel like you got betrayed, to feel angry? It's not natural to say, "God is good," when something difficult happens.

We have to practice this stuff.

There has to be a regular practice of, *I gotta trust You in this, I gotta trust You in this*. It's not natural to lay all anxiety down. It's natural to dwell on what's false, to dwell on the lie. That's what's natural for human beings. So it takes practice. Romans 12 says that we are transformed by the renewal of the mind. I mean, that's how serious this practice is. My mind always goes to what's dishonorable. It just does. I think of when someone cuts me off in traffic; often I immediately respond as if he did it on purpose. I don't grant him the mercy to assume he was just aloof and wasn't paying attention. I imagine that the guy saw me in his mirror and thought, *I'm just going to jack with that guy.*

That imagined scenario just comes out of me! I don't even have to think about it. Which is why Paul tells us specifically to intentionally think on better things, things that line up with Christ and His gracious gospel.

We'll conclude with this return of Paul's: "I rejoiced"—there's that word again—"in the Lord greatly that now at length you have revived your concern for me. You were indeed concerned for me, but you had no opportunity" (Phil. 4:10).

What's going on here? The gaps are starting to fill in. The maturing Christians who make up the church at Philippi are actually walking in all that Paul's taught them up to this point, thinking of him as greater than themselves, loving him, humbling themselves, and even reaching out to him. In fact, he says that they wanted to do it. It wasn't dutiful obligation but rather "concern."

Here is what has happened: the postal service wasn't all that reliable back in the day. You could write a letter. You would try to send an offering. Then you'd get shipwrecked, caught up in a war, ambushed, or robbed. The Philippians wanted to help Paul all along and weren't able to—but now he hears about their love for him. The open heart he demonstrated for them is being recipro-cated. Paul is overjoyed at the thought of it. He's rejoicing greatly. In what? That his old friend Lydia, that the sweet slave girl, that his old jailer have been growing into the maturity of affection, love, passion, and care for him. And that they are still passionately pursuing Jesus.

As with Paul, for the Philippians to live is Christ and to die is gain. It was the power of God that did this in them. And Paul doesn't need to waste any worry on them any longer.

CHAPTER ELEVEN

CHRIST IS ALL

I know how to be brought low, and I know
how to abound. (Phil. 4:12)

We often hear in weddings that the bride and groom will be together:

> For better or for worse,
> For richer or for poorer,
> In sickness and in health.

These are lovely sentiments that most of us incorporate into our wedding vows, promising to stay in covenant with our spouses no matter what life brings our way. We commit then, at the start of our journey together, to stick together until the very end.

The problem is that when I promised my wife that I'd stay with her through better and worse, richer and poorer, and health and sickness, in the back of my mind I thought that "better" would be awesome and "worse" would never really be that bad. I figured we might not ever be exceedingly rich, but we'd never really be that poor either. We might not be in perfect health our whole lives, but neither of us would ever get some kind of disease or end up in some debilitating, disfiguring accident.

Very few of us actually think that the worst will happen to us. We put our hope in the better and mitigate any thoughts of the worse. We think that we will live our lives with some nice upsides and some minor setbacks—nothing more. We think that the extreme circumstances are just that—extreme. A few people might experience extreme circumstances, but not many.

This, to be sure, is not the testimony of Paul. When a man like Paul goes through some wild swings in life, from ridiculous highs to extreme lows, it makes sense that we'd give him our attention. We should examine how he handled such polarities and see what kind of counsel he offers us. Because the reality is, these circumstances we like to call "extreme" happen to more of us more often than we like to admit. If Paul can honor Christ through all that he endured, surely we in our (usually) minor swings of high to low can keep the faith.

Right?

PAUL'S GOSPEL-SHAPED LIFE

There are three kinds of preachers who hold our attention. First, there are people you listen to because something about the way they communicate resonates with you. So you'll listen to them because while they teach, their style is engaging, dynamic, or captivating. Maybe they're charismatic in personality. Next there are people you will listen to because they possess a wealth of knowledge, and their exegesis is impeccable. They can teach the Scriptures extremely well, and you know you're learning a lot. Finally, there are people whose lives have been so filled with both the pinnacles of joy and the valleys of sorrow that you're drawn to them simply because of the amount of life they've lived.

We once had a guest come speak at The Village who was, honestly, not the best communicator in the world. But members of his family had been killed in the Rwandan genocide, and he spoke to us about the nature of forgiveness and how one forgives atrocities such as genocide. It wasn't his dynamic speech or his exegesis, and it wasn't that he was so good with the Scriptures that he drew us in and we listened and paid attention. It was simply that he lived his life, and the depths of his experience radiated wisdom.

Of course, in the most perfect scenario possible, you get to listen to a speaker who is dynamic and engaging, intelligent and enlightening, and full of life experience and personal history—all in one "package." We'd all love to know somebody who doesn't just take you to the Bible and show you where God says something but can take you to the Bible and show you where God says something while at the same time pointing back to a particular point in his own life where he experienced God's declaration to be true or especially transformative.

We may not know such a person personally on this side of heaven, but we have a friend like that already, one who speaks through the power of the Holy Spirit. In this chapter, we will take a look at some episodes in Paul's life and see that what he writes in Philippians and his other letters is not simply the fruit of knowing the information of the gospel, but also the fruit of having lived a life captured by the gospel.

We will resume with this passage, which includes one of the most "famous" verses in the Bible:

> I rejoiced in the Lord greatly that now at length you have revived your concern for me. You were indeed concerned for me, but you had no opportunity. Not that I am speaking of being in need, for I have learned in whatever situation I am to be content. I know how to be brought low, and I know how to abound. In any and every circumstance, I have learned the secret of facing plenty and hunger, abundance and need. I can do all things through him who strengthens me. (Phil. 4:10–13)

Most of us aren't going to be able to say what Paul says here—at least not without some heavy-duty life experience. What Paul says is that he has "learned" that Christ is enough. He has learned to know that Jesus is his satisfaction both in a full belly and in a growling stomach.

The truth is that the majority of us will not swing between these two poles all that often. Some of us have an abundance: wealth, steak, caviar, or whatever. Maybe you're eating mac 'n' cheese or Ramen noodles occasionally. Even if we can't eat the steak and caviar all the time, nearly all of us in the first world eat three meals a day, or we could if we wanted to. Most of us don't have to wonder where our next meal will come from. Most of us will grumble about it, but we can usually afford to put some gas in our car. Money might be tight, but we don't live in poverty.

But Paul is saying here, "I've been poor. I've been hungry." And that is odd enough compared to our typical life experience, but the more astounding thing he says is this: "I learned to be content in those situations."

Paul is an interesting man. He's a Roman citizen, but he's a Jew. And not just an average Jew. He has serious Jewish cred, remember? "Circumcised on the eighth day, of the people of Israel, of the tribe of Benjamin, a Hebrew of Hebrews; as to the law, a Pharisee" (Phil. 3:5).

Paul, whose original name was Saul, has learned the Pharisaical code, learned the law inside and out, and distinguished himself as an up-and-comer. He's essentially a phenom. He's from a good family. He's bold and aggressive. Everybody who's anybody in the Pharisaic organization knows Saul. And he's from Tarsus, so he's a city boy, an intellectual, and, on top of that, both passionate and brilliant. He basically develops the reputation as the next big deal.

Then *the Way* breaks out. Jesus is crucified and apparently is resurrected from the dead. Saul gets very frustrated by this perversion of Judaism. So he listens to one of these Christians, a man named Stephen, and he hears him preach and teach Christ crucified and resurrected. As he listens, Saul begins to burn with anger, and he's not the only one. The whole crowd gets irate. The crowd decides that they should handle Stephen by killing him. So they drag him down and begin to pelt him with rocks until he dies. Some of them, I guess, can't get a good enough range of motion while they're pelting Stephen, so they take their jackets off—but they don't want to throw their garments, their outer garments, down on the ground. So instead they lay them at the feet of Saul. So Saul holds the coats of the men who are killing Stephen, and the Bible is very clear in the book of Acts that Saul heartily approves of what is occurring.

The Bible says that after Stephen's martyrdom, the church begins to spread out. They leave Jerusalem, but they leave preaching the Word wherever they go. And Saul chases them. He passionately pursues Christians because he wants to kill more of them. When he says in Philippians 3:6 that he was zealous to persecute the church, he means it. It was his driving force. He was purpose driven to eradicate the church.

Eventually he gets assigned to go to Damascus. He has heard that some Christians there are preaching the gospel and that more people are starting to believe in Jesus. So Saul takes to his horse and assembles a group of soldiers, and they all head to Damascus. But on the way, Jesus hijacks Saul's plan, and a vision of the glorious Christ confronts him.

The effect is not gentle. Jesus blinds him and then speaks to him: "Saul, Saul, why are you persecuting me?"

Saul says, "Who are you?"

Jesus says, "I am Jesus, whom you are persecuting" (Acts 9:4–6).

Saul wanders into Damascus and finds his way to a man named Ananias.

I love the interaction between God and Ananias because God basically says, "Hey, Saul of Tarsus is here. I want you to go heal him." And Ananias reminds God, "Um, he's come here to kill me. How about we not heal him? I like him blind and hurt" (see Acts 9:10–14).

God's response to Ananias does not bode well for the rest of Paul's life. God tells Ananias, "No, no, no. Go and heal him, because I will show him how much he must suffer for My name" (see Acts 9:15–16).

Ananias obeys and, calling Paul "brother," lays hands on him and prays for him. The Bible says that scales fell off Paul's eyes (Acts 9:17–18). Now a transformed believer in Christ, having been waylaid by the gospel, Paul is baptized and ready to begin a new life of faith.

Right out of the gate in Acts 9, just days after his conversion, Paul takes to the pulpit and preaches his first sermon. And, believe it or not, *it goes well*. He confounds the Jews, according to Acts 9:21. They can't argue with him. Has that ever happened to you? It's not that the person you're arguing with just talks so much that they wear you out, but that they substantively dismantle every one of your arguments so that you have literally nothing else to say. Paul did that to his former comrades.

Now the believers in Damascus—Ananias and all the others—
think, *Man, this guy is amazing.* This has to feel good to Paul. I
mean, if you've ever stumbled onto a gift you didn't know you
had, surprised to just find it one day suddenly popping up, you
know it feels amazing. So Paul keeps preaching, and things are
going well. But by the end of Acts 9, his old friends, the ones with
whom he had done life, stayed up late talking about the law, gone
to church—the ones he'd built his life around, the people he'd
invested in and knew like family—all turned on him. His friends
tried to murder him (Acts 9:23).

Paul went from high to low in the blink of an eye.

I just can't imagine what it's like to go to bed at night when you've
had to flee a city for fear that your own friends will murder you.

Paul leaves Damascus. When he arrives in Jerusalem, the
Christians there won't receive him. They are afraid of him (Acts
9:26). So now, not only has Paul been betrayed by his old friends,
but his new friends won't receive him. They won't have anything to
do with him. Can you imagine how lonely it would feel if, when
you turned your life over to the Lord, your old friends rejected
you and no new friends accepted you? That is an unreal depth of
loneliness.

Finally, a man named Barnabas, a great encourager, befriends
Paul (Acts 9:27). So Paul goes from a low to a high. He has come
out of a very traumatic and miraculous experience only to enter a
world of rejection—until suddenly one brave Christian soul says
to the others, "You guys can be afraid. I'm going to love on him."
And Paul and Barnabas become very good friends.

It's not too long after this that a group of Greeks enter a debate with Paul about how the universe works. Paul preaches the gospel to them, and once again, he is so good and intellectually powerful, he stumps them. And these guys do what every group that ran out of arguments wanted to do: *they try to kill him* (Acts 9:28–29). So right after enjoying an important friendship, he's under threat of murder. Again.

I think it's difficult for us to get our minds around that. Maybe you've been through a whirlwind life like this. I know it happens. I know people who've had massive ups and downs like this, out of trauma into comfort and back into some horrific experiences. I don't want to be naive about that. However, I don't think most of us can honestly say we know what it's like to be faced with people wanting to murder us. I certainly don't. And this isn't a one-time shocking experience for Paul. *This is his life.* It's going to happen over and over and over again.

Now the Hellenists want to kill him, and the Bible says that Paul starts unpacking the gospel for a man named Sergius, who is also a pretty brilliant guy. As Paul shares the good news with Sergius, a demon-possessed man named Bar Jesus begins trying to distract them, yelling and doing whatever he can to keep Paul from sharing the gospel. For the first time in Paul's life, Paul casts out a demon; he rebukes Bar Jesus, which leaves the man blind and mute (Acts 13:6–11). I don't know how arguments go where you're from, but in my world, if what you say to a guy leaves him where he can't see or speak—*you won.*

Paul is now walking in power. This is no longer just an intellectual exercise for him. This is not just an educational reasoning from the Old Testament that Christ is the Messiah; Paul wields immense spiritual power, and Sergius, of course, becomes a believer.

Paul is on a mountaintop again. But his story isn't over.

Paul takes the mission to Lystra, and right away, in the middle of a sermon, a stone flies in from the back of the room and slams into the side of his head. So he glances up, and then another stone sails in—and another stone and another stone and another. And he thinks, reasonably, *I'm going to die today*. In the past, he's been on the other side of this sort of thing. He's been the one throwing the stones. So he knows how this thing ends.

Those persecuting him think they've killed him. They drag him out of the city, thinking he is dead, and leave him there (Acts 14:19). They don't want him to rot inside the city limits. This would be a point lower than low, wouldn't it?

Supernaturally, however, Paul rises. They haven't killed him. He lives to preach another day.

But just ahead lies a strong disagreement between Paul and Barnabas, his good friend, and they go their separate ways (Acts 15:36–40). Paul's been stoned, and now he's alone again, with not even a friend with whom he can commiserate.

He eventually reaches Philippi. And it's there that he finds a Bible study where a wealthy woman named Lydia comes to know the Lord in a pretty powerful way. Lydia says, "Hey, come live with our family for a while." So Paul and his fellow missionaries, who have basically been transients, find themselves living in the mansion of the CEO of Prada. I would say that's a good day.

I've been to places in Asia where the mattresses are pieces of plywood, and I've been in our California king-sized bed with a pillow top. And although I'll do either for the glory of God, I do have a preference! I'll take the pillow top, please. That's what I like.

I'm picturing Paul at Lydia's house now. Do you think Lydia might have had a chef? I don't know. I'm guessing that Lydia, if she's got the kind of money we think she does, probably isn't microwaving mac 'n' cheese. I'm thinking maybe there's a chef in her house. I'm guessing this is a good day for Paul, another enjoyable high.

It doesn't last very long, because a race riot breaks out just a couple of days later. Stuck in the middle of it, Paul gets arrested, tortured, and thrown into jail. He ends up in Thessalonica, in Iberia, and makes many converts, but there is also a group of Jews there that hate him. They seriously hate him. They hate him so much, they start to follow him wherever he goes. It doesn't matter what city he visits. It doesn't matter where he heads. They follow him. They are not going to attack him directly; instead, what they do is stir up crowds, agitating others against Paul. They rouse a mob wherever Paul goes and push the mob to attack him.

In Acts 17 they follow him into Athens. They mock him while he's preaching. Paul is an intellect among intellects. There are smart guys, and then there are guys who make smart guys look dumb. Paul is one of those guys who makes smart guys look dumb, and when he's teaching in Athens, the other guys stand around and jeer and laugh.

The boys from Thessalonica show up, so Paul goes into Corinth and preaches the gospel to the ruler of the synagogue, a guy by the name of Crispus who becomes a convert. The ruler of the synagogue becomes a believer in Jesus Christ (Acts 18:8).

Again, Paul has gone from high to low and low to high. The swings of better and worse keep coming.

Now, while Paul is in Corinth with all of this trauma fresh on his mind, and after having been beaten and imprisoned and rejected and laughed at, the Word of the Lord comes to him. God says, "Do not be afraid, but go on speaking and do not be silent, for I am with you, and no one will attack you to harm you, for I have many in this city who are my people" (Acts 18:9–10). After the crowd from Thessalonica has followed him from place to place, once Paul's in Corinth, God says, "Stay, preach, no one will harm you." After Paul's been beaten with rods, tortured in prison, stoned and left for dead, I would think this word would come like cool water in a desert place.

However, Paul is only being prepared for more missional adventures. The gospel works in Ephesus in such a powerful way that the weirdest things imaginable begin to occur. We find out that Paul's handkerchief and apron are healing people (Acts 19:11–12). So people are literally stealing his clothes, wiping his clothes on people, and watching those people be healed. God's moving so powerfully that people who aren't even believers are trying to get in on the supernatural stuff (v. 13).

Ephesus is where the story of the seven sons of Sceva takes place. These guys see Paul cast out a demon and think to themselves, *Oh, we've got to do this.* So they go find a demon-possessed guy. Where you find those guys, I don't know. But they find one and start messing around with exorcism, saying and doing what they think Paul was saying and doing. They say, "In the name of Jesus Christ, Paul's god, I command you to come out" (Acts 19:13, author's translation).

And the demon speaks. I love what the demon says. (Probably the only time I'll ever say this.) He says, "I know Jesus Christ. And I've heard of Paul" (Acts 19:15, author's translation). I've always loved the fact that the demon has heard of Paul, like there is this network of communication in the demon world. But the next line is great: "But who are you?" (v. 15).

We read then that the demon turns on them and beats them both bloody and naked (Acts 19:16). I like that part, too, because I've said for years that if you come into a fight with pants and you're no longer wearing pants when the fight's over, you lost the fight. It's kind of like the aforementioned axiom: you know you lost if you end up blind and mute. I don't care if you got a good headlock in. I don't care if you decked him once in the eye. If you came into the fight with drawers and you're no longer wearing drawers when the fight was over, you lost.

Eventually in Ephesus, the gospel has so penetrated the culture that the whole socioeconomic climate of the city begins to change. There are men who have made hundreds of thousands of dollars creating golden images. They've made idols—false gods. But the gospel has so captured the hearts of people in the community that nobody buys the idols anymore. So these men have to shut down their shops (Acts 19:23–27).

What happens when somebody's putting you out of business? You get angry. And these idol makers start a riot and stir up a lot of animosity toward Christianity—and its messenger, Paul.

Ephesus was an unbelievable high. If you've ever been part of a Christian community in a smaller-sized city, maybe you've gotten together with believers from all over the area and talked about what it would look like if the gospel were to take over. Maybe you prayed together earnestly for revival in your city for a long time. You prayed that God would revitalize the place, pour Himself out on it in a fresh way. I don't know if you've ever been a part of anything like that, but it happens quite a bit all over the place. There are people in cities everywhere who've been praying regularly for years, decades even, for revival in their area. And it happened in Ephesus. It wasn't just a group of people coming together and asking for it. God actually did it in Ephesus.

As the spiritual transformation begins to negatively affect those who profited from idolatry in Ephesus, about forty men make an oath that they will not eat or drink anything until Paul is dead (Acts 23:12–15). You know, it's one thing to say, "I wish that guy would die." It's quite another thing to say, "I'm not eating until I kill that guy." Forty people agree to that vow. I just get a mean email, and I'm like, "Why don't they like me?" Paul has large groups of people committed to his annihilation.

That's a dark day.

Paul testifies without fear, and he's arrested. As they're taking him to Rome, he is testifying about Jesus Christ all along the way.

Paul starts to run down the catalog of lows in his life in 2 Corinthians 11:

> I repeat, let no one think me foolish. But even if you do, accept me as a fool, so that I too may boast a little. What I am saying with this boastful confidence, I say not as the Lord would but as a fool. Since many boast according to the flesh, I too will boast. For you gladly bear with fools, being wise yourselves! For you bear it if someone makes slaves of you, or devours you, or takes advantage of you, or puts on airs, or strikes you in the face. To my shame, I must say, we were too weak for that!
>
> But whatever anyone else dares to boast of—I am speaking as a fool—I also dare to boast of that. Are they Hebrews? So am I. Are they Israelites? So am I. Are they offspring of Abraham? So am I. Are they servants of Christ? I am a better one—I am talking like a madman—with far greater labors, far more imprisonments, with countless beatings. (vv. 16–23)

Which means what? He has been beaten so many times for the cause of Christ that he lost count. Personally, I can remember my beatings. Those are things I tend to remember. But Paul has suffered "countless beatings, *and often near death*" (2 Cor. 11:23).

Some of his beatings left him nearly dead; in fact, he says this happened *often*. He continues:

> Five times I received at the hands of the Jews the forty lashes less one. Three times I was beaten with rods. Once I was stoned. Three times I was shipwrecked; a night and a day I was adrift at sea. (2 Cor. 11:24–25)

I'm just going to be straight with you: if I'm on a boat with Paul twice and we go down both times, I'm not getting on a third boat with him. If you live through a plane crash, maybe you'd say, "Well, you know, let's just get back on that plane," but if *that* plane went down, you wouldn't be getting on another plane. Or if you do, you should have to wear a T-shirt that reads, "Planes crash when I'm on them," so the rest of us can see that and opt out.

Paul is shipwrecked three times and once finds himself adrift at sea for twenty-four hours. He keeps going:

> On frequent journeys, in danger from rivers, danger from robbers, danger from my own people, danger from Gentiles, danger in the city, danger in the wilderness, danger at sea, danger from false brothers; in toil and hardship, through many a sleepless night, in hunger and thirst, often without food, in cold and exposure. And, apart from other things, there is the daily pressure on me of

my anxiety for all the churches. Who is weak, and
I am not weak? Who is made to fall, and I am not
indignant? (2 Cor. 11:26–29)

But look at his perspective on this whole venture in suffering: "For
the sake of Christ, then, I am content with weaknesses, insults,
hardships, persecutions, and calamities. For when I am weak, then
I am strong" (2 Cor. 12:10).

CHRIST THE CENTER

With that brief biographical overview, we see in Paul a man who
begins life affluent, an up-and-comer, the next big thing, and ends
up—to borrow his own phrasing—"counting all of that as rubbish"
and enduring all the lows we just chronicled. What he writes in
Philippians 4 gleams with deeper resonance against that background.

Hold in your mind not just Paul relaxing at Lydia's house,
eating steak, not just Paul confounding his opponents or casting
out demons or enjoying the glory of God's miraculous wonders.
Hold in your mind his being scourged, having the flesh torn from
his back. Hold in your mind his struggling to keep his head above
water as the ship he's on sinks violently into the watery abyss. Hold
in your mind his restless sleep at night while thugs scour the streets
to find him and kill him. Hold in your mind the vision of his body
crumpled on the ground, face in the bloody dirt, covering his head
and body in a desperate bid not to die from the seemingly unend-
ing onslaught of stones.

Now read this again:

> Not that I am speaking of being in need, for I have
> learned in whatever situation I am to be content.
> I know how to be brought low, and I know how
> to abound. In any and every circumstance, I have
> learned the secret of facing plenty and hunger,
> abundance and need. I can do all things through
> him who strengthens me. (Phil. 4:11–13)

Do you see now how Philippians 4:13 is not about chasing your dreams, following your passion, pulling yourself up by your bootstraps, accomplishing anything you want with God's help? It is instead the testimony of those who have Christ and have found Him supremely valuable, joyous, and satisfying. In a life constantly marked by these extreme highs and lows, Paul has found the great constant security, the great centering hope: Jesus Christ Himself.

Is there a more misquoted verse in the Bible than Philippians 4:13? I don't think there is. I think people want to apply that to everything. A Christian businessman might say, "I'm going to be a CEO. I can do all things through Christ who strengthens me."

Well, that's kind of a swing and a miss. That's *really* out of context.

When I was a teenager, there were these Christian T-shirts that had pictures of athletes on them with the caption underneath, "I can do all things through Christ who strengthens me." I wonder what exactly this conveyed to the kid who always struck out.

There are things that I just can't do. Right? This verse isn't evidence that I can do whatever I want. Now, can Christ do the miraculous? Absolutely. But this text isn't saying that you can be a major league ball player through Christ. This is not what Paul's saying at all. He's saying that if you are in the big leagues, then praise His name, and if you're too weak to even lift the jug to be the team's water boy, praise His name.

You can't take Philippians 4:13 and make it mean you can do anything you want. That's not what Paul is saying. In context, he is saying, "I've learned to be content when I received everything I want; I learned to be content when I got nothing I wanted. I can do either one by the power of Christ."

When Paul says, "To live is Christ, and to die is gain," he means it. *If you want to kill me, I will be more than fine: I will get to be with Jesus. My death will be filled with Christ. And if you want to let me live, I will press on in mission. My life will be filled with Christ. If you want to torture me or imprison me or mock me, I will trust in God. My suffering will make me like Christ. I will see it as a sharing of His own suffering.*

Through highs and lows, better and worse, richer and poorer, sickness and health, you can do all things through Christ who strengthens you, when Christ becomes your all. A gospel-shaped life fills every space it takes with unconquerable faith and unfailing love. If you are united in Christ through His gospel, you are then as secure as Christ is. In fact, according to Jesus, even if they kill you, you won't die (John 11:26).

More than likely, there is no one reading this book who has consistently in life experienced these extreme polar opposites as

Paul did. But consider his life. There is something profoundly helpful about looking at his life, being aware of what he lived through, walked through, and seeing how God sustained him through all of it. My hope is that in the future, every time you open up your Bible and read one of these letters—Ephesians, Philippians, Colossians, or 1 and 2 Timothy—you might be struck not just by the fact that they are God's Word, but that this man lived those words out. Paul's not just blowing smoke. When he says you can be content regardless of your circumstances, he knows what he's talking about!

What about you? As we continue to look for "developmental deficiencies" in our maturation in Christ, how are you doing in the area of contentment? How quick is your impulse to find satisfaction in Christ, to go to the joy of the gospel in times of stress, frustration, disappointment, and trouble?

CHAPTER TWELVE

TRUE CONTENTMENT

The grace of the Lord Jesus Christ be with your spirit. (Phil. 4:23)

One of the more astounding things Paul says as he closes his letter to the Philippians is easily missed. He writes about desiring the church to increase in their affections for him, desiring them to send love his way. He's expressed gladness that they've done so. He's written about how God has supplied contentment for him in every situation he's gone through, and he's about to reiterate that same idea. Then, in the midst of all that, we find this deceptively profound phrase: "Not that I am speaking of being in need" (Phil. 4:11).

Paul has adopted the revolutionary position that he has no needs. All his needs have been met in Jesus, so all he has left are wants. He is honest about what he wants, but even those are shaped by his satisfaction in Christ. Paul is not perfect, and he never claims to be, but he has "learned," remember, that when he is starving, suffering, imprisoned, and even denying, he still has everything, because he has Christ. If Christ is all, and if he has Christ, then he really has no needs.

Can you handle that?

Can we agree that in Christ we have no need for anything? We need to be totally sanctified and glorified, yes, but in Christ those are foregone conclusions we just haven't received yet. We have them even if we don't actually experience them quite yet. They are ours. Paul further along in the passage says, "And my God will supply every need of yours according to his riches in glory in Christ Jesus" (4:19).

When I was a kid, video games as we know them today had basically just been invented. The only video-game console we knew about was called Atari. It was a little black square with a black stick on it and one orange button. Can you imagine that? One button. Every game on the Atari console (all three of them) made the same sound. It was a type of beeping and ringing that would make you lose your mind if you played for too long.

Back in those days, you could play outside until the street light came on, and you didn't have to think to yourself, *I should go outside and play.* You just did it. You got home, you did your homework, and you knew your parents did not want you in the house. So you'd go play outside.

Sports had seasons. Baseball had a season. There was a football season. There was a basketball season. You didn't travel all over the state, playing ice hockey in Texas. You just didn't do it. The world didn't work like that.

I know it sounds crazy, but cartoons were on in the morning, right after school, and on Saturday mornings. That's it. I tried to convince my daughter, and she doesn't believe me. She thinks I'm lying to her. We had no Cartoon Network. You couldn't watch a four-hour block of SpongeBob SquarePants at seven thirty on Tuesday night. That's not how the world worked.

No one had a cell phone. You *might* have a pager, and it was the size of a loaf of bread. And if you had it on vibrate it would break your hip.

Movies came out a few per month, not four or five new ones every weekend.

We didn't have remote controls when I was a kid. That's why people had children. There was a little sliding bar that sat on top of the television, and you had to get up when Dad told you and slide it over. Some of you probably had to turn one of the two massive knobs on the set instead.

That's how the world worked. And in my childhood, we were already far advanced compared to the generation before us!

All these years later, the world is such a different place. For instance, if you want popcorn right now, you throw a bag in the microwave and press a button that says *popcorn*. How George Jetson is that? Just press the popcorn button, and you get popcorn. When I was a kid, you had to buy a bag of kernels, pour oil in a pan, and put the kernels in there. You had to mess with grease and an open flame!

Why is it so important for us to understand contentment as we come to the end of our walk through Paul's letter to the

Philippians? We live in a world where there is more to do than there has ever been in the history of mankind. There are more things to see, more places to go, and easier means to get there. We live in the most entertained world that humanity has ever experienced, and yet most of us are bored out of our minds and frustrated.

Contentment is unbelievably important in this world. Not just happiness—but *contentment*. And here is what Paul has said, absent all the conveniences of the modern world and in all the suffering of the ancient one, "I don't need anything. I've learned to be content" (Phil. 4:11, author's translation).

LEARNING CONTENTMENT

Paul says he "learned ... to be content" (4:11); he "learned the secret" (4:12). And if a guy who is blameless as to the law (3:6) has to learn contentment, clearly we've got some learning to do too.

Contentment is not natural. We have to learn it, and there are two ways we can do that learning. It is not evident in the English translation of Philippians 4, but Paul is actually unpacking it that way in the Greek. There are two different ideas here. One is that Paul is learning in the intellectual sense; he is learning the rules of contentment. He has learned mentally, as (hopefully) you are learning right now as you read this, that "this is how to be content." Where would Paul learn this? From the Scriptures.

Paul is able to get into Habakkuk 3 and read the prophet:

Though the fig tree should not blossom,
    nor fruit be on the vines,
the produce of the olive fail
    and the fields yield no food,
the flock be cut off from the fold
    and there be no herd in the stalls,
yet I will rejoice in the LORD;
    I will take joy in the God of my salvation.
GOD, the Lord, is my strength;
    he makes my feet like the deer's;
    he makes me tread on my high places. (vv.
    17–19)

Paul has certainly also read David's song in Psalm 63:3: "Your steadfast love is better than life"—and in Psalm 4:7: "You have put more joy in my heart than they have when their grain and wine abound."

Paul can read and learn contentment from what he sees in the Scriptures. He can see in the Bible that God is better than food or shelter. He learns that God is better than life. Most of us, actually, learn contentment primarily that way.

But Paul comes back to the idea of learning contentment. The first time in 4:11 corresponds to that sense of learning we just covered, the intellectual sense, and now in 4:12 he repeats himself: "I have learned the secret." Now he's talking about learning in the experiential sense. He has, by experience, learned the lesson he knew intellectually.

Paul has learned to be content by living in Lydia's house with all of the abundance and opulence. He was able to sit in the midst of that and still love Christ, follow Him, and know that He is better.

You might say, "Well, of course he learned contentment in a place of abundance." But you'd not be thinking of it in the right way. What Paul was able to do was enjoy the abundance for what it was, as a gift from God for a time, but contentment means being satisfied not with the gifts but with the Giver. And this makes all the difference. A failure to understand this distinction is why it is so hard for rich people to follow Jesus. Because money doesn't satisfy—but so many of those with lots of wealth think they will reach contentment if they just get "more." But "more" is a desire that never ends. This is why Gary Thomas calls contentment a "discipline." It's something that has to be recalled, practiced, put into effect in every circumstance. In his book *Authentic Faith*, Thomas writes about a family vacation:

> When we visited Knott's Berry Farm, an amusement park with a frontier theme, there were virtually no lines, and we went easily from major attraction to major attraction, in many cases walking right on. If the kids really enjoyed the ride, they stayed on and rode again.
>
> My then six-year-old daughter Kelsey was having the time of her life. After about three hours, however, I noticed something curious. She

jumped off some little cars; earlier, she had ridden a train, a log ride, a Ferris wheel, a flying school bus—you name it. Her words, however, revealed a spirit that was getting *more* hungry, not less: "What's next?" she asked, with a slightly desperate edge to her voice.

That's when I realized there's never enough excitement to quiet the human heart. We'll never have as much excitement as we want. This has been true from the beginning of time.[1]

The dissatisfaction, the idolatrous desire for "more," is in the mutated DNA of our fallenness. And it will be there until our hearts are full with Jesus. As Augustine says, "Restless is our heart until it comes to rest in thee."[2] God set it up this way, making sure that the accumulation of satisfactions other than Him will *never* satisfy.

According to Stephen Altrogge:

We *won't* be fully satisfied when we get what we want. Because God loves us and wants us to find our satisfaction in him, he won't allow us to be satisfied. To believe that we'll finally be happy when we get what we want is a lie.[3]

And of course the true test of our satisfaction with Christ is not simply our contentment with "more" but our contentment with "less." Paul showed his contentment in the abundance of Lydia's house by demonstrating his willingness to walk away from all of it in a heartbeat, because he believed that Christ was better than those things.

He's not saying, "I've learned to live life like a wealthy man." He's saying, "I've learned to live for Christ in wealth. I didn't sell out for wealth. Wealth did not become my god. I didn't hold tightly to material possessions. I didn't hold tightly to my comfort."

Paul could give a testimony of contentment that might sound like this: "Lydia's chef blew up a medium-rare filet. It melted in my mouth. It was amazing. And the next day, I left. I cast the demon out of a little girl, and I slept the next night in prison after I got beaten and thrown in the stocks. I know how to live in opulence and not sell out to it. And I know how to live impoverished, to have nothing, to be imprisoned, and not give over to despair in it."

The secret Paul learned both intellectually and experientially, and the secret he is now passing on to the Philippians and to us—*to you*—is this: true contentment is not in any way related to circumstances. True contentment is tuned to the deeper reality of the gospel and God's kingdom.

If the Lord brings wealth, praise the Lord. I'm going to use that wealth to push the kingdom forward, to glorify Christ, to serve Him completely. Openhanded, I will say, "All is yours."

If it's poverty, if it's nothing, praise the Lord. Openhanded, I will trust Him to provide everything I need to be all that He's asked me to be. Either way, I'm all good. It does not matter what befalls me, good or bad. It doesn't matter if everyone loves me or everyone hates me. It does not matter if I'm healthy or sick. It does not matter if everything works like I want it to or if nothing does. I have learned to be content in everything. I learned it from God's Word, and I have learned it from God's providence.

A couple of years ago, I visited Asia and got really, really sick. We were not going into a very safe area—we'd been briefed about potential arrest and bodily harm—so I was already uneasy, but by the time we landed, I was horrifically sick, and my situation just got worse and worse. By the eighth day of our mission, I hadn't eaten anything. I couldn't keep any liquid down. I'd developed sores all over my mouth from throwing up. I'm not sure I can adequately describe how absolutely miserable I was. I lost eighteen pounds. I don't really have eighteen pounds to lose.

I didn't get out of bed. I just laid there with nothing, no control, no way to get better, no hospital to go to, nothing.

Do you want to know something? In that experience might have been some of the sweetest, deepest, most beautiful interactions I've ever had with the Lord. I'm telling you, there was a point there when I didn't think I was coming home. There were a couple of moments in which I thought, *I'm going to die on this nasty couch.* Honestly, if that was God's will, I just wanted Him to speed up the process. I didn't want it to get dragged out another eight days. But in the midst of that suffering, I had some good, deep, serious talks with God, and He was very, very sweet to me in the power of His Spirit.

So now when I'm home, where I've got a king-sized bed, a nice house, beautiful daughters, a strong son, a fantastic wife, a great church, awesome friends, money in the bank, any food that I want—all the riches of first-world abundance I could ask for and a bunch more besides—I am content. I have learned that when I'm thirteen hours away from my family, sick to death, and in the midst of a dangerous culture for Christians, I know the love of God and true contentment.

Don't get me wrong—I'm so grateful over here! To this day, eating a meal at my house is just a worshipful experience for me. My young daughter says a little prayer, and then my boy throws his hands up and says, "Amen!" We eat slowly. We laugh. It's a great thing. But, then, over there, in the midst of thinking I might die—that was a great thing. Because I had Jesus.

Circumstances don't matter. "To live is Christ, and to die is gain." The message of Philippians is that life is lived for Him, to Him, through Him, with Him, about Him, and in Him. That's where Paul goes once again. As in Romans 16, he cannot help but exult, can't help but sing! "To our God and Father be glory forever and ever. Amen" (Phil. 4:20).

Rejoice, rejoice, rejoice. God is big enough, beautiful enough, strong enough, lovely enough, perfect enough, sustaining enough in any circumstance.

Wherever you are, He is with you, always.

RICHES IN GLORY

We learn contentment from God's Word and its application to our hearts as we walk with Him through the highs and lows of life.

We learn contentment not by primarily learning coping skills or response strategies in times of difficulty and adopting ambivalence in times of comfort, but rather by learning just how all-surpassingly good our gracious God really is. Paul's point is not summarized in the learning of advice or a set of helpful skills; his point is summed up in *knowing God.*

If you just know God, have a sense of His depth of love and abundance of grace all for you in Christ, you'll consequently find wealth appropriately unimpressive and suffering appropriately untroubling.

This is how Paul closes his important words to his friends in Philippi:

> Yet it was kind of you to share my trouble. And you Philippians yourselves know that in the beginning of the gospel, when I left Macedonia, no church entered into partnership with me in giving and receiving, except you only. Even in Thessalonica you sent me help for my needs once and again. Not that I seek the gift, but I seek the fruit that increases to your credit. I have received full payment, and more. I am well supplied, having received from Epaphroditus the gifts you sent, a fragrant offering, a sacrifice acceptable and pleasing to God. And my God will supply every need of yours according to his riches in glory in Christ Jesus. To our God and Father be glory forever and ever. Amen.

> Greet every saint in Christ Jesus. The broth-
> ers who are with me greet you. All the saints greet
> you, especially those of Caesar's household.
>   The grace of the Lord Jesus Christ be with
> your spirit. (Phil. 4:14–23)

At least we get another reminder that Paul is not some spiritual superhero. Despite his declared contentment in comfort and
suffering, in life and death, he nevertheless says in verse 14, "Still,
it was nice that you cared about me."

He would have been satisfied in Christ if they hadn't, but he's
not so heavenly minded that he's unable to say thank you to his
friends for reaching out. In acknowledging their efforts, he once
again commends their maturity, lavishing his praise on them for
the way they passionately pursue Christ.

William Hendriksen elaborates:

> Paul is careful not to leave the impression that
> the gift had been superfluous and that he did not
> appreciate it. On the contrary, he indicates that
> he was definitely pleased with it. Hence, he says,
> *Nevertheless, you did nobly in sharing my affliction.*
> It was, says Paul as it were, *a noble, a beautiful
> deed*, like that of Mary of Bethany (Mark 14:6).
> Had the Philippians not been true sympathizers,
> so that they felt Paul's affliction as if it were their
> very own, they would not have performed their

generous deed. The gift indicated that they had made common cause with Paul's affliction, were true sharers in it. Truly, the *fellowship* (see on Phil. 1:5) was operating beautifully![4]

The church's beauty shines through. They, as Paul says in Philippians 2:15, shine like lights in the world. They demonstrate their heavenly citizenship (3:20). Because of this, Paul reminds them that they will be fully repaid in the glory to come. God's riches are inexhaustible, and they are all for all of His children. As the father in the parable of the lost son says to his legalistic son, "You are always with me, and all that is mine is yours" (Luke 15:31).

The Philippians learned to live like this is true. Paul praises them for this and urges them on all the more, alluding to the vast supply of heavenly satisfaction that, while no less real this very moment, waits in a storehouse for that day rapidly approaching. God will supply all their needs (not their wants, necessarily, but their needs) according to His riches (not theirs, but His, which are better) in glory in Christ Jesus. God will not ask anything of you now, in other words, that He will not pay you back for infinity-fold in the day to come. Not because He owes you a thing, but because He loves you and is gracious beyond measure.

The Second Advent is coming. The Incarnation is the first advent. At that time, the Jewish people were waiting on the Messiah, and the Messiah came and died on the cross, purchasing sinful souls and absorbing God's wrath so all that was under God's wrath ultimately disappears. There is victory over death now.

Death has no sting, no victory. Disease has lost its power. Christ purchased all of that in the cross. There are eternal riches in that.

Now we live between the two advents in what theologians would call the "already and the not yet," or "the narrow place." So it's already paid for, but it has not yet been consummated

The day is coming when Christ will return, and the Bible makes that great day of the Lord a pretty scary event for most of humanity. Most of humanity will want mountains to fall on them to hide them, and there will be no place to hide. Every act of treason, every act of rebellion, every errant word, every bit of wickedness, every bit of self-exaltation, every bit of narcissism, every act that communicates, "Forget You, God. I'm smarter than You," will be laid bare before you and God.

If we look at this from a biblical perspective, godlier, more righteous people than you and me will ever be have seen God face-to-face and fallen on the ground, absolutely terrified. Isaiah, who was an upright man of God, sees God, falls on the ground, and says, "Woe is me!" (Isa. 6:5). The same word is used later when Jesus says over and over to the Pharisees, "Woe to you" (Matt. 23:13–36). Isaiah is saying, "Woe is me." *Why?* "For I am a man of unclean lips, … [and] my eyes have seen the King" (Isa. 6:5). So one glance at Jesus Christ, at God enthroned, and Isaiah falls on the ground and is terrified and says, "Woe is me." John, according to tradition, is boiled alive and doesn't die and also, for the record, doesn't recant. He doesn't say, "We made it all up." He doesn't die, so they exile him to Patmos. He sees Jesus in a vision and falls on the ground like a dead man.

Therefore, you and I, probably on any plane you want to lay down—moral, intellectual, or spiritual—are not in the same league as Isaiah or John. And yet, both of them see God and are terrified. The day is coming when God's patience will be all used up. He will pour out His abounding love on the elect, and it will be over. And when that happens, He's going to crack the sky, He's going to come back to judge, and all that we have done will be revealed. There will be no place to hide. There will be no lies that work. Every motivation will be exposed.

Basically, the file drawer opens up, and every wicked thought and every wicked action will be held up for examination. And on that day, we're going to want a substitute, a champion. On that day, we are going to want someone to declare, "I took care of that. I paid for that. It is paid in full."

Paul teaches that mature Christians are serious about the things of God and pursue God seriously, because when Christ is revealed in all His glory, we want to be raised with Him. We want *all* the riches. We want Him with us always. We don't want a life-sized salvation; rather, we want an eternity-sized salvation. So we don't stop at conversion; we press on. Because we want to make it evident that we believe someone is going to step in at that final moment and say, "I paid for that. I absorbed that. What was due for that, I paid for it all, not according to their riches but according to Mine."

Christian, if you have been raised with Christ, is there a seriousness in you about the things of God? Are you legitimately pursuing Him, growing into the fullness of Him? If your mind is set on Him, how does that work itself out in your life?

It's so easy in the church to gloss over such questions, to assume by our proximity to the community of faith and the teaching of the gospel that we are immersed personally in the pursuit of Christ. We can become content in ourselves and not experience the holy discontentment that would push us to find true contentment according to God's riches in Christ instead of the paltry riches of religion or playing church games.

How are you going about having your mind transformed and your heart stirred up for the things of God? And if the answer is nothing, then I have to wonder what you really are looking at, staring at, and chasing after.

Maybe you ought to repent right now.

I wonder if Paul might have exposed some of your games with God simply through your reading of the book of Philippians.

I fear some of us have been in church so long and learned "Christianese" and how to act right and how to give all the Sunday school answers, and still we've never applied any of those answers to our own lives. I wonder how many of us will be serious about the fact that there will be a day in which the glory of Christ will shine in its fullness and we will be held to account. And on that day we want to be raised with Him. On that day, we will want our contentment in Him to explode in the infinite joy of heaven.

For the last two thousand years, this whole Christianity thing has *just happened*. What I mean is, Paul goes into Philippi and Lydia the wealthy CEO comes to know the Lord, but so does the little slave girl, and so does the jailer. These unlikely converts mature in their faith, and as they mature in their faith, they share the gospel with others so that the great gospel—God reconciling men and women to Himself despite their sin, through the finished work of Christ—grows and grows and grows. It spreads into nation after nation, across tribal and linguistic and ethnic boundaries, and spans generations upon generations. Over the last two thousand years, it spread throughout the ancient world into Asia down into Africa, across to the Western world, finding its way into the Americas, into New England and the northeast United States, and then across the entire nation.

I live in Dallas, Texas. Do you know how the gospel got to Dallas, Texas? If you trace it back, the gospel got here because the apostle Paul went into Philippi, went into Ephesus, went into Corinth.

If the gospel can do *that*, it can certainly stir up your affections for Him. Certainly it can captivate your mind and speak into your heart. If the gospel can transform the world and holds in its powerful reach the promise of eternal life, certainly it can transform you this very day, and day by day, until that ultimate day you join with the saints to receive the supply of all your needs according to God's riches in glory with Christ Jesus.

You right now can join not only the apostle Paul but countless millions of others throughout history and still to come, all of whom will say:

"I count it all loss next to the surpassing greatness of Jesus Christ, my Lord."

To live truly is Christ. And to die is incomparable, infinite gain.

NOTES

CHAPTER ONE: ODD BEGINNINGS

1. Richard Sibbes, *A Bruised Reed* (ReadaClassic.com, 2010), 5.

2. Saint Chrysostom, *Saint Chrysostom on the Priesthood, Ascetic Treatises, Select Homilies and Letters and Homilies on the Statues,* ed. Philip Schaff (Whitefish, MT: Kessinger Publishing, 2004), 14.

CHAPTER TWO: THE WORTHY LIFE

1. D. L. Moody, quoted in William R. Moody, *The Life of Dwight L. Moody* (Grand Rapids, MI: Fleming H. Revell, 1900), iii.

CHAPTER FIVE: THE PASSIONATE PURSUIT

1. Augustine, *Confessions,* second edition, translated by F. J. Sheed, edited by Michael P. Foley (Indianapolis: Hackett, 2006), 163.

2. Martin Luther, quoted in James Kellerman, trans., *Dr. Martin Luthers Werke* (Weimar: Hermann Boehlaus Nachfolger, 1909), 513.

3. Charles Spurgeon, *The Works of Charles Spurgeon,* "October 15" (MobileReference, 2010).

4. John Owen, "The Explication of the Text; John 17:24," *The Works of John Owen,* Volume 1, edited by William H. Goold (Edinburgh: T. & T. Clark, 1862), 291.

5. Brother Lawrence, *The Practice of the Presence of God* (Grand Rapids, MI: Spire Books, 1967), 37.

CHAPTER SIX: OWNED

1. Helen Howarth Lemmel, "The Heavenly Vision," 1922. Public domain.

CHAPTER EIGHT: CENTERING ON THE GOSPEL

1. Martin Luther, *A Commentary on St. Paul's Epistle to the Galatians* (London: Mathews and Leigh, 1807), 58.

2. D. A. Carson, *Basics for Believers* (Grand Rapids, MI: Baker, 1996), 93.

CHAPTER NINE: REJOICE?

1. Jud Wilhite, *Torn* (Colorado Springs: Multnomah, 2011), 148–49.

CHAPTER TEN: NO WORRIES

1. Joe Thorn, *Note to Self* (Wheaton, IL: Crossway, 2011), 127.

2. Michael Kelley, *Wednesdays Were Pretty Normal* (Nashville: Broadman and Holman, 2012), 208–9.

3. John Phillips, *Exploring Ephesians and Philippians: An Expository Commentary* (Grand Rapids, MI: Kregel, 1995), 169–70.

CHAPTER TWELVE: TRUE CONTENTMENT

1. Gary Thomas, *Authentic Faith* (Grand Rapids, MI: Zondervan, 2002), 175.

2. Saint Augustine of Hippo, *The Confessions of St. Augustine* (Mineola, NY: Dover Publications, 2002), 1.

3. Stephen Altrogge, *The Greener Grass Conspiracy* (Wheaton, IL: Crossway, 2011), 55–56.

4. William Hendriksen, *New Testament Commentary: Philippians* (Grand Rapids, MI: Baker, 1953), 207.